HYMNS
FROM
THE DASAM GRANTH

Edited by
Prof. Gobind Singh Mansukhani M.A. Ph. D

Hemkunt

© Hemkunt Press 1980
First Published : 1980
Sixth Revised Edition : 1997
Seventh Edition : 2004

ISBN 81-7010-180-8

Published by :

Hemkunt Press
A-78, Naraina Industrial Area, Phase-I, New Delhi-110028
Tel.: 2579-2083, 2579-5079, 2579-0032 Fax: 91-11-2611-3705
E-mail: hemkunt@ndf.vsnl.net.in
Website: www.hemkuntpublishers.com

Some Hemkunt Books on Sikhism
For Children
Illustrated in four colours and black and white
The Story of Guru Nanak
Life Story of Guru Gobind Singh
Life Story of Guru Nanak
The Story of Maharaja Ranjit Singh
Stories from Sikh History I–VII
Sikh Studies I–VII

For Adults
Japji
Hymns from Guru Granth Sahib
Hymns from the Dasam Granth
(In above three books text in Gurmukhi and Roman scripts and meanings in English)
Introduction to Sikhism
Encyclopedia of Sikhism
Bhagat Bani in Guru Granth Sahib
The Holy Granth – Shri Guru Granth Sahib Vol. I

Printed at : Hindustan Offset Press, A-26, N.I.A., Phase-II, N.D.-28

FOREWORD

This book is a companion-volume to the earlier publication entitled **Hymns from Guru Granth Sahib**.

The seventy hymns selected have been thoughtfully arranged under different sections—on God, the Holy Name, False Religion, Transitory World, Universal Brotherhood, the Khalsa, Yoga, Supplication and about Himself. The compositions on God cover both His positive and negative aspects. Hypocrisy and ritual are exposed under the heading of False Religion. The hymns on the Transitory World and the Holy Name respectively show the contrast between the ephemeral and the permanent. The hymns on Universal Brotherhood emphasise the egalitarian aspects of the Guru's philosophy. The hymns on Yoga show how the Guru's Sahaj-Yoga differs from the traditional Yoga. The hymns on the Khalsa sum up the characteristics of the ideal man and the Guru's appreciation of His devotees. The last section containing extracts from **Bachitra Natak** and **Zafar-Namah** – both autobiographical hymns throw light on the Guru's mission and his willingness to pay any price for the vindication of Truth, Freedom and Justice.

The editor has covered all the aspects of the Tenth Guru's personality and teaching. Some of the hymns in this collection are quite popular and are sung in Sikh institutions and congregations.

These hymns throw light mainly on the two aspects of the Guru's character. He was not only a Prophet but also a saint-warrior. Though his heart was full of the milk of human kindness, he wielded the sword fearlessly to uproot the tyrant and the wicked. He firmly believed that there is a moral order in the universe, where Good must prevail over Evil in the end.

I feel confident that the book will be a source of great enlightenment and edification to the readers. It meets a long-felt need and will be welcomed by the English-knowing people.

Baisakhi Day
13th April, 1980

Gurdial Singh Dhillon
Formerly, Director
Guru Harkrishan Public School
Vasant Vihar, New Delhi

PREFACE TO THE REVISED EDITION

HYMNS FROM THE DASAM GRANTH contains seventy hymns of the tenth Guru. Each hymn is reproduced in the original Punjabi text and underneath is the transliteration in Roman-English, for the benefit of those who cannot read Punjabi. On the opposite page is the English translation, line by line. In the foot-note, I have given annotations on difficult words and concepts.

The Dasam Granth edition in the Punjabi script available in the market, contains 1428 pages. The compositions are in Brij Bhasha, Hindi, Punjabi and Persian languages, and are printed in the following order.

Jaap, Akal Ustat, Bachitra Natak, Chandi Charitar I & II, Chandi Ki Var, Gian Prabodh, Chaubis Avtar, Shabad Hazare, Savaiye, Khalsa Mehma, Shastra Nam Mala, Triya Charitra, Zafar Namah and Hikayat.

The Dasam Granth was compiled by Bhai Mani Singh on the instructions of Guru Gobind Singh's widow – Mata Sundri in 1711. Scholars have not agreed that all the compositions of the Dasam Granth are from the pen of the Tenth Guru. However, the Sikh Panth has accepted the entire Dasam Granth as the work of Guru Gobind Singh.

The present work has been arranged under various headings: God, Holy Name, False Religion, Transitory World, Universal Brotherhood, the Khalsa, Yoga and Autobiographical. Suitable hymns have been presented to throw light on the above themes. The Tenth Guru exposed the hollowness and futility of ritual, Yogic penance and hypocrisy. On the other hand, he valued the Brotherhood of man, Meditation on the Holy Name, Sacrifice for the preservation of Truth and Justice, and living according to the ideal of the Khalsa. His values have stood the test of time and provide a basis for the progressive survival of mankind.

An introduction to the Dasam Granth has been added. The author acknowledges his debt to the translations of Dr. Gopal Singh, Bhai Jodha Singh and annotations of Bhai Randhir Singh.

London
April 1988

Gobind Singh Mansukhani

INTRODUCTION TO THE DASAM GRANTH

The Dasam Granth is the second Holy Book of the Sikhs. There are three versions of the work, namely : Bhai Mani Singh's Bir, Patna Sahib Bir and Sangrur Bir. Giani Kartar Singh has mentioned nine lithographic and printed editions. The most acceptable edition is the Sri Guru Granth Sahib Ji Dasam Patshahi, published by Munshi Gulab Singh & Sons, Lahore, in Sambat Guru Nanak 444 (1913 A.D). This edition has 1399 pages of 19 lines each. The popular printed edition available today has 1428 pages. The total number of verses is 17,155.

Its Contents

Jap Sahib : This contains 199 verses which praise the attributes of God. More than 900 names have been used for the Lord; some are positive, others are negative. For example, the first quotation contains both positive and negative aspects of God, while the second contains only negative ones:

(i) "I salute that God who is Unborn:
I salute that Lord who is most Beautiful." (21)

(ii) Formless, Peerless, Beginningless, Birthless,
Bodyless, Colourless, Desireless, Dauntless." (30)

Akal Ustat : This is one of the finest works of the Tenth Guru. The title "Akal Ustat" means "Praise of the Immortal Lord. " Here, the Guru uses new names for God like Sarabloh (All-steel), Sarab-kal (All-death), Kharag-ketu (with a banner decorated by the imprint of the sword). This God is the embodiment of fearlessness and courage. The Guru rejects the idea of any chosen people, that is any group being favoured by the Lord – the Jews, the Muslims, the Christians. The Akal Ustat includes Ten Swayyas found in the *Nitnem*. The Guru rejected idol-worship and also the traditional marks of symbols of holiness. He emphasised repeatedly the brotherhood of man and the need for serving our fellow-men .

Bachitra Natak : The title means 'The wonderful drama', it is a 'Drama of Life'. It includes details of the Guru's life and wonderful performances of legendary deities and popular heroes. The Guru begins the work with an invocation to "The Sword"– one of his Symbols for God.

Chandi Charitra : This details of battles of Chandi with various demons. Apart from the standard version of Chandi in Bachitra Natak which is based on Bhagwat Puran, there are two other versions in Hindi, based on Markande Puran.

Chandi-di-var : Also called Var Sri Bhagauti Ji Ki is in Punjabi and contains 55 verses. It is regarded as the first Var of its kind in Punjabi.

Gian Prabodh : This contains stories from the Mahabharata and also some pithy sayings and aphorisms. It is a book of practical wisdom, explaining the essence of Raj-Dharam (political morality), Dan-Dharam (the principles of charity), Bhog- Dharam (the principles of family-life), and Moksh-Dharam (the code for salvation).

Chaubis Avtar: Though technically a part of Bachitra Natak, it is also treated as an independent composition. Here are given the 24 incarnations of the Hindu god Vishnu. There is also a supplement called *Mehdi-Mir-Badh*, which gives an account of the Saviours who came to uphold truth and justice.

Brahma Avtar : Like Chaubis Avtar, but dealing with the seven incarnations of Brahma followed by descriptions of eight kings. It contains 343 verses.

Rudra Avtar: Deals with the two incarnations of Indra, namely as Datta Avtar and Paras Nath Avtar.

Shabad Patshashi Dasvee : This is a collection of ten hymns (Shabads, also called Shabad Hazare). They are for singing in the classical raga indicated for each Shabad. They deal with the futility of asceticism, idolatry and attachment. One hymn in the *Khayal* tells us of the Guru's condition after escape from Chamkaur to the Machhiwara jungle. In this, Guru declares his faith in the essentiality of God, to care for the Children.

Sri Mukh Vak Swayyas : These are 32 quatrains on God and current religious practices. The Guru rejects the ritual and hypocrisy of all priestly classes.

Khalsa Mehma : These are verses in praise of the Khalsa brotherhood.

Pakhyan Charitra or Charito-pakhyan : These are 404 stories in verse, illustrating the noble and wicked sides of life. Some deal with bad women, some with their virtue and valour. The total number of verses is 7558.

Sri Shastra Nam Mala : This is a list of armaments, and deeds of those who used them well. The names of the weapons are spelt in the form of riddles.

Zafar-Nama : It is actually the reply of Guru Gobind Singh to Aurangzeb's letter to the Guru to meet him at the Moghul Court. It is written in Persian verse and in two parts, the first being an invocation to God to seek His blessing, and the second, the actual reply to Aurangzeb. The Guru gives a fair criticism of the emperor, mentioning both his good and bad qualities. The Guru emphasised the moral law that all who are hypocritical and violent will eventually get their just punishment, for the wheel of providence grinds slowly and exceedingly small.

Hikayat : These are eleven stories in Persian verse, each with a moral lesson. Some of the stories are the same as in Pakhyan Charitra. These stories begin with the praise of God.

The Dasam Granth was primarily compiled to awaken heroic sentiments among the Sikhs so as to enable them to fight against political injustice and religious intolerance. The influence of Hindu theology, history, mythology, philosophy and literature on Guru Gobind Singh is quite evident. The book also serves as a reference work on all classical allusions found in the Adi Granth. It has therefore an important place in Sikh literature and theology.

The compositions of the Dasam Granth may be divided into two main categories :

(i) *Devotional Poetry* : like Jaap, Akal Ustat, Benati Chaupai, Shabad Hazare, etc.

(ii) *Heroic Poetry* : like Chaubis Avtar, Bachitra Natak, Chandi-di-Var, etc.

Devotional Poetry : Apart from the praises of God which include more than a hundred positive attributes of Him in the *Jaap*, the Guru dwells on the negative and destructive aspects of God. Weaponry or warfare is the way in which He punishes the wicked and the unjust. The Martial God is All-steel, the Holder of the Sword, the User of the Bow and the Arrow. The Guru emphasises too the efficacy of the Holy Name. He says :

"Repeat God's Name, establish God's Name in your heart :

Do obeisance to the Lord and repeat His Name."

As a saint-soldier, Guru Gobind Singh declared his mission in the following words :

"I assumed birth for the purpose of spreading the Faith, Protecting the saints and extirpating all tyrants."

"When all peaceful methods fail,
It is righteous to draw the sword."

"Knowing me to be His slave, God has aided me.
He has taken me by His hand and saved me."

In *Chandi-di-Var*, the Guru has emphasised the role of the sword wielded by Rama, Krishna and Durga, for the defeat of evil forces.

In *Krishan Avtar*, Guru Gobind Singh has expressly, mentioned the objective of his poetry thus : "I have rendered in the Tenth Chapter of the Bhagwat, with no other purpose than to arouse desire and zeal for waging a holy war, a righteous vindication of the Lord." The Guru wanted to acquaint the Sikhs with the Indian religious lore and to rouse their conscience against tyranny and injustice, as also to remove their sloth, frustration and cowardice.

Courage and Victory, are the Guru's watchwords. He says :

"Even if a low coward hears the ballad (of Chandi), he will be thrilled with the love of war and offer himself for fight in battle."

The Guru's praise of the sword is in fact his praise of God. Just as the sword subdues enemies, so does God defeat the wicked. In this sense, Sword is God, and God is Sword.

Music

The following *Ragas* and *Raginis* are indicated in the compositions noted below. The number of hymns is mentioned in small brackets.

			Shabad Hazare			
1. Bilaval	[Rag]		(1)			
2. Devgandhari	[Ragini]	" "	(2)	and Paras Nath	(2)
3. Kalyan	[Ragini]	" "	(1)	"	(1)
4. Khayal	[Style]	" "	(1)		
5. Ramkali	[Ragini]	" "	(3)	"	(2)
6. Sorath	[Rag]	" "	(1)	"	(12)
7. Tilang-Kafi	[Mixed]	" "	(1)	"	

8.	Adana	[Rag]	...	...	"	(1)
9.	Basant	[Rag]	...	...	"	(1)
10.	Bhairav	[Rag]	...	...	"	(1)
11.	Dhanasri	[Ragini]	...	...	"	(1)
12.	Gauri	[Ragini]	...	...	"	(2)
13.	Kafi	[Ragini]	...	...	"	(5)
14.	Kedara	[Rag]	...	...	"	(1)
15.	Maru	[Rag]	...	...	"	(3)
16.	Paraj	[Ragini]	...	...	"	(3)
17.	Sarang	[Rag]	...	...	"	(6)
18.	Suhi	[Ragini]	...	...	"	(3)
19.	Tilang	[Rag]	...	...	"	(1)

The musical notes are at times martial, at times peaceful and soothing. We have both secular and sacred music in this Granth. The poet and the singer in the Tenth Guru join hands together to offer beautiful pictures and patterns in melody.

Diction

Guru Gobind Singh used Punjabi, Brij, Arabic and Persian words which suited the theme and the mood. Sanskrit words dominate the devotional compositions. Sometimes he used words from dialects like Dingal (Rajasthan) and Avadhi (Patna). As a conscientious artist in words, his semantic diversity is amazing. Onomatopoeic words and rhythmic syllables are found in plenty, as for instance, the cawing of the crows – *Kah Kah su Kookat Kan Kiyan.*

The importance of the Dasam Granth is three-fold. Firstly, it is a source of material on the life and work of Guru Gobind Singh, particularly the two autobiographical compositions–*Bachitra Natak* and *Zafar Nama.* Historians have drawn largely on these poems for their authenticity. *Secondly,* it is a treasury of lyrical poetry, portrait-painting, heroic and narrative poetry. *Thirdly,* it is a collection of literature in Brij Bhasha, Punjabi and Persian, belonging to the later medieval India. It also offers a glimpse into ancient Indian history, folklore and culture. It is a panorama of thousands of years of Indian tradition and civilisation—the procession of princes and paupers, the learned and the ignorant passing on the stage in strange costumes, exhibiting the frailties and inhibitions of mortal man.

Guru Gobind Singh was a prolific poet. At Paonta Sahib, where most of his literary activity took place, he employed 52 poets who worked for him in creative writing and translation. Being occupied by his wars with the hill-chiefs, the Moghul emperor and local governors, he had no time to compile a book of his own compositions. Later, when some one suggested that he include some of his own hymns in the Adi Granth, he rejected the suggestion, saying that his compositions were not his serious work, that he was merely experimenting with poetry and music, this humility being responsible for the non-incorporation of his hymns in that Scripture.

Mata Sundri, the widow of Guru Gobind Singh once asked Bhai Mani Singh to compile a volume of the Guru's poetry. She handed over to him all the copies she possessed of his poems. Bhai Mani Singh also collected copies from others. Bhai Mani Singh, who was a relative and had been a close companion of the Guru, spent many years sifting the materials and finally compiled a volume known as The Granth of the Tenth Master or the "Dasam Granth", in 1721.

The Dasam Granth embodies the philosophy and mission of Guru Gobind Singh. The Guru's philosophy has both positive and negative aspects. On the positive side, it declares the supremacy of God and His moral law. He uses, the power of the sword against the negative forces, of tyranny, violence and bigotry. His heroic poetry is meant to inspire, not to entertain. It is a poetry of higher ethics, aesthetically fulfilling and spiritually gratifying. Above all, it gives a clear picture of the real world, without any gloss or blackening. In the opening scene of *Hussaini Jung* (1695), his words are like the blows of a hammer:

"Goaded by the tumultuous booming of drums,
The doughty warriors gave a thunderous roar.
They jumped and leapt with their zeal afire and all intent.
As they plied their weapons with great excitement, inflicting grievous wounds." (Bachitra Natak)

On the other hand, the Guru's caustic criticism of meaningless ritual, greed and hypocrisy of so-called holy men; is vivid and compelling.

There is both imagery and resonance – an aesthetic vibration, which goes far beyond the literal meaning of words.

The heroic strain–*Bir rasa* - end in the tranquility of the *Shant rasa* (feeling of peace). The Guru's insight into the psychology of lovers in the portrayal of Radha's mind bypasses the traditional erotic detail. "Man's nature has an exterior world and also an interior world that lies within him. With his outer or conscious personality, man deals with the empirical world, with his inner personality, he struggles with the problems of his own individuality; few men know more than a few fragments of their inner world which is the unconscious, or of lying in the darkness of unknowing. The unconscious part of human nature is the source and origin of the conscious, of all created things and manifestations, even of creation."

Guru Gobind Singh was a fine singer and musicologist. He used new ragas like *Adana, Kafi* and *Paraj,* which were not included in the Adi Granth. His use of *Khayal* was also an addition to Sikh Sacred Music. The Guru patronised musicians. Buddhu and Saddu who were *rababis* sang the Asa-di-var in his court. He used poetry for both secular and spiritual purposes. His heroic poetry was intended to end the traditional concept of non-violence – *Ahimsa* – then forced on people by both king and priest. Now the voice of conscience should inspire people to fight for freedom and justice. His devotional poetry was intended to inspire the people for spiritual attainment. One writer has remarked:

"He gave us musical form that was martial and hymnal, sacred and secular, simple and complex. In him, we find a saint singing spiritual songs, a soldier listening to martial music, a householder singing of the virtue, of leading good life and of a painter creating wonderful sound pictures in music."

Finally, as the bulk of Guru Gobind Singh's poetry in the Dasam Granth is in Brij-bhasha, he is considered as a great poet not only in Hindi literature but also for his achievements in Punjabi and Persian poetry.

CONTENTS

SECTION I : GOD

		Page
1.	Chakar Chihan	18
2.	Gobinday mukanday	20
3.	Ajai, Alai, Abhai	22
4.	Namastul Pranaamay	24
5.	Akaal Purakh	26
6.	Jalay Hari, thhalay Hari	28
7.	Dinan kee	30
8.	Ketay Indra	32
9.	Faarsee firangee	34
10.	Kaam na Krodh na	36
11.	Rogan tay ar sogan tay	38
12.	Naarad say	40
13.	Khag Khand	42
14.	Pah gahay	44
15.	Prabhjoo	46
16.	Bin Kartaar	48
17.	Kewal Kaalaee	50
18.	So kim	52
19.	Ik bin	54
20.	Jo kah	56
21.	Kiyo kah	58
22.	Khandaa Pritham	60
23.	Sat sadev	62

SECTION II : HOLY NAME

24.	Praani Param	64
25.	Bin Har	66
26.	Kahay ko	68
27.	Bed Kateb na	70

SECTION III : FALSE RELIGION

28.	Sravag sudh	72
29.	Teerath Naan	74

30.	Kahaa bhaiyo	76
31.	Teerath kot	78
32.	Kaahoo lai	80
33.	Jo Jug tai	82
34.	Jaal badhay	84
35.	Kaal gayo	86
36.	Bed Kateb parhay	88
37.	Jo Jugiaan	90
38.	Aakhan bheetar	92
39.	Fokat Karam	94

SECTION IV : TRANSITORY WORLD

40.	Matay matang	96
41.	Jeet firay	98
42.	Sudh sipaah	100
43.	Beer apaar	102
44.	Manav Indra	104
45.	Jitay Raam	106
46.	To tan	108

SECTION V : UNIVERSAL BROTHERHOOD

47.	Kou bhaiyo	110
48.	Dehura masit	112
49.	Jaisay ek	114

SECTION VI : THE KHALSA

50.	Jaagat jot	116
51.	Dhan jio	118
52.	Judh Jitay	120
53.	Sev karee	122

SECTION VII : YOGA

54.	Ray man aiso	124
55.	Ray man ih	126
56.	Dhian Lagaai	128

SECTION VIII : AUTOBIOGRAPHICAL

57.	Tinn Bediyan	..	130
58.	Tilak janjoo	..	134
59.	Ab mai	..	136
60.	Ih kaaran	..	138
61.	Hum eh kaaj	..	140
62.	Murpita poorab	..	142
63.	Jabai Baan	..	144
64.	Sarab-kaal sabh	..	146
65.	Mitr piyaray	..	148
66.	Bibaayad tu	..	150

SECTION IX : SUPPLICATION

67.	Deh Siva	..	152
68.	Hay rav, hay sas	..	154
69.	Hamaree karo	..	156
70.	Prithum Bhagauti	..	158

HYMNS
From
THE DASAM GRANTH

1. ਜਾਪ ॥

ਸ੍ਰੀ ਮੁਖਵਾਕ ਪਾਤਿਸ਼ਾਹੀ ੧੦ ॥ ਛਪੈ ਛੰਦ ॥ ਤ੍ਵ ਪ੍ਰਸਾਦਿ ॥
ਚੱਕ੍ਰ ਚਿਹਨ ਅਰੁ ਬਰਨ ਜਾਤਿ ਅਰੁ ਪਾਤਿ ਨਹਿਨ ਜਿਹ ॥
ਰੂਪ ਰੰਗ ਅਰੁ ਰੇਖ ਭੇਖ ਕੋਊ ਕਹਿ ਨ ਸਕਤਿ ਕਿਹ ॥
ਅਚਲ ਮੂਰਤਿ ਅਨੁਭਵ ਪ੍ਰਕਾਸ ਅਮਿਤੋਜ ਕਹਿੱਜੈ ॥
ਕੋਟਿ ਇੰਦ੍ਰ ਇੰਦ੍ਰਾਣਿ ਸਾਹੁ ਸਾਹਾਣਿ ਗਣਿੱਜੈ ॥
ਤ੍ਰਿਭਵਣ ਮਹੀਪ ਸੁਰ ਨਰ ਅਸੁਰ ਨੇਤਿ ਨੇਤਿ ਬਨ ਤ੍ਰਿਣ ਕਹਤ ॥
ਤ੍ਵ ਸਰਬ ਨਾਮ ਕੱਥੈ ਕਵਨ ਕਰਮ ਨਾਮ ਬਰਨਤ ਸੁਮਤਿ ॥੧॥

1. JAAP*

Sri Mukhwak Patshahee Dasvee, Chhapai Chhand, Tav Prasaad

Chakr Chihan ar baran jaat ar paat nahin jih,

Roop rung ar rekh bhekh kou kah na sakat kih,

Achal moorat anubhav prakaas amitoj kahijai,

Kot Indra Indraan Saah Saahaan ganijai,

Tribhavan maheep sur nar asur,

net net ban trin kahat,

Tav sarab naam kathai kavan karam Naam barnat sumat.   (1)

---

*Where "aa" is used, it should be pronounced as 'ਆ' as in father.

SECTION I
GOD

1. Jaap

God hath no mark, feature, sect, caste or sub-caste.

No one can say about his appearance, colour, figure and dress.

God is eternal, self-illumined and omnipotent.

He is greater than millions of Indras[1] and is considered the King of kings.

He is the Lord of the three worlds of gods, men and demons;

The woods and the plants proclaim his infinitude

None can count all His Names; the wise can call Him by His doings. (1)*

---

1. Indra is the King of Heaven, also god of rain.
* The number at the bottom of each page of this book refers to the page of the Dasam Granth edition which consists of 1428 pages.

2. ਜਾਪੁ ॥

ਚਾਚਰੀ ਛੰਦ ॥ ਤ੍ਵ ਪ੍ਰਸਾਦਿ ॥

ਗੁਬਿੰਦੇ । ਮੁਕੰਦੇ । ਉਦਾਰੇ । ਅਪਾਰੇ ॥ ੧ ॥ ੯੪ ॥
ਹਰੀਅੰ । ਕਰੀਅੰ । ਨ੍ਰਿਨਾਮੇ । ਅਕਾਮੇ ॥ ੨ ॥ ੯੫ ॥

ਭੁਜੰਗ ਪ੍ਰਜਾਤ ਛੰਦ

ਚੱਤ੍ਰ ਚੱਕ੍ਰ ਕਰਤਾ । ਚੱਤ੍ਰ ਚੱਕ੍ਰ ਹਰਤਾ ।
ਚੱਤ੍ਰ ਚੱਕ੍ਰ ਦਾਨੇ । ਚੱਤ੍ਰ ਚੱਕ੍ਰ ਜਾਨੇ ॥ ੧ ॥ ੯੬ ॥
ਚੱਤ੍ਰ ਚੱਕ੍ਰ ਵਰਤੀ । ਚੱਤ੍ਰ ਚੱਕ੍ਰ ਭਰਤੀ ॥
ਚੱਤ੍ਰ ਚੱਕ੍ਰ ਪਾਲੇ । ਚੱਤ੍ਰ ਚੱਕ੍ਰ ਕਾਲੇ ॥ ੨ ॥ ੯੭ ॥
ਚੱਤ੍ਰ ਚੱਕ੍ਰ ਪਾਸੇ । ਚੱਤ੍ਰ ਚੱਕ੍ਰ ਵਾਸੇ ॥
ਚੱਤ੍ਰ ਚੱਕ੍ਰ ਮਾਨਯੈ । ਚੱਤ੍ਰ ਚੱਕ੍ਰ ਦਾਨਯੈ ॥ ੩ ॥ ੯੮ ॥

2. JAAP

Chachri Chand, Tav Prasaad

Gobinday, Mukanday, Udaray, apaaray, 94
Hareean, Karaean, Nirnaamay, akaamay. 95

Bhujang Prayat Chhand

Chatra, Ckakra Kartaa, chatra chakra hartaa,
Chatra, ckakra daanay, chatra chakra jaanay 96
Chatra, chakra vartee, chatra chakra bhartee,
Chatra, chakra paalay, chatra chakra kaalay 97
Chatra chakra paasay, Chatra chakra vaasay
Chatra chakra maaniyai, chatra chakra daaniyai, 98

2. JAAP

Chachri Chhand Tav Prasaad

The Master of the earth. Liberator. Compassionate. Infinite. 94

The Destroyer. The Doer. Without a name. Without desire. 95

Bhujang Prayat Chhand

He is the Creator of four directions and also the Destroyer,
Who is Compassionate in all directions, and whom every side acknowledges (as its own). 96

Who directs and fills all directions, and projects and sustains all, and then destroys all. 97

Who is present on all sides, who exists in every corner, whom everyone acknowledges and who gives to all. 98

3. ਜਾਪੁ ॥

ੲਕ ਅੱਛਰੀ ਛੰਦ

ਅਜੈ। ਅਲੈ। ਅਭੈ। ਅਬੈ॥੧॥੧੮੯॥
ਅਭੂ। ਅਜੂ। ਅਨਾਸ। ਅਕਾਸ॥੨॥੧੯੦॥
ਅਗੰਜ। ਅਭੰਜ। ਅਲੱਖ। ਅਭੱਖ॥੩॥੧੯੧॥
ਅਕਾਲ। ਦਿਆਲ। ਅਲੇਖ। ਅਭੇਖ॥੪॥੧੯੨॥
ਅਨਾਮ। ਅਕਾਮ। ਅਗਾਹ। ਅਢਾਹ॥੫॥੧੯੩॥
ਅਨਾਥੇ। ਪ੍ਰਮਾਥੇ। ਅਜੋਨੀ। ਅਮੋਨੀ॥੬॥੧੯੪॥
ਨਾ ਰਾਗੇ। ਨ ਰੰਗੇ। ਨ ਰੂਪੇ। ਨ ਰੇਖੇ॥੭॥੧੯੫॥
ਅਕਰਮੰ। ਅਭਰਮੰ। ਅਗੰਜੇ। ਅਲੇਖੇ॥੮॥੧੯੬॥

3. JAAP

Ek Achhari Chhand

Ajai, Alai, Abhai, Abai. 189
Abhoo, Ajoo, Anaas, Akaas. 190
Aganj, Abhanj, Alakh, Abhakh. 191
Akaal, Dayaal, Alekh, Abhekh. 192
Anaam, Akaam, Agaah, Adhah. 193
Anaathay, Parmaathay, Ajoni, Amoni. 194
Na raagay, na rangay, na roopay, na rekhay. 195
Akarmang, Abbaramang, Aganjay, Alaykhay 196

3. JAAP

Ek Achhri Chhand

Unborn. Undying.
Of fear free. Ever the same, 189

Not cast into the womb,
Nor destroyed ever,
(Who vaults, all over, like) the sky. 190

Unbreakable. Unpierceable.
Unknowable. Undissolved. 191

Beyond Time. Compassionate.
Unaccountable. Without a garb. 192

Without a name. Without desire.
Profound and Uncorroded. 193

Not dependent, the Destroyer of all.
Subject neither to transmigration,
Nor to silence. 194

Uninvolved, without colour,
Without form, without sign. 195

Unaffected by deeds. Without doubt.
Unaccountable, and Indestructible, 196.

4. ਜਾਪੁ

ਭੁਜੰਗ ਪ੍ਰਯਾਤ ਛੰਦ ॥

ਨਮਸਤੁਲ ਪ੍ਰਨਾਮੇ ਸਮਸਤੁਲ ਪ੍ਰਣਾਸੇ ॥
ਅਗੰਜੁਲ ਅਨਾਮੇ ਸਮਸਤੁਲ ਨਿਵਾਸੇ ॥
ਨਿਕਾਮੰ ਬਿਭੂਤੇ ਸਮਸਤੁਲ ਸਰੂਪੇ ॥
ਕੁਕਰਮੰ ਪ੍ਰਣਾਸੀ ਸੁ ਧਰਮੰ ਬਿਭੂਤੇ ॥੧੯੭॥
ਸਦਾ ਸਚਿਦਾਨੰਦ ਸਤ੍ਰੰ ਪ੍ਰਣਾਸੀ ॥
ਕਰੀਮੁਲ ਕੁਨਿੰਦਾ ਸਮਸਤੁਲ ਨਿਵਾਸੀ ॥
ਅਜਾਇਬ ਬਿਭੂਤੇ ਗਜਾਇਬ ਗਨੀਮੇ ॥
ਹਰੀਅੰ ਕਰੀਅੰ ਕਰੀਮੁਲ ਰਹੀਮੇ ॥੧੯੮॥
ਚੱਤ੍ਰ ਚੱਕ੍ਰ ਵਰਤੀ ਚੱਤ੍ਰ ਚੱਕ੍ਰ ਭੁਗਤੇ ॥
ਸੁਯੰਭਵ ਸੁਭੰ ਸਰਬਦਾ ਸਰਬ ਜੁਗਤੇ ॥
ਦੁਕਾਲੰ ਪ੍ਰਣਾਸੀ ਦਇਆਲੰ ਸਰੂਪੇ ॥
ਸਦਾ ਅੰਗ ਸੰਗੇ ਅਭੰਗੰ ਬਿਭੂਤੇ ॥੧੯੯॥

4. JAAP

Bhujang Prayaat Chhand

Namastul pranaamay, samastul pranaasay,
Aganjul anaamay, samastul nivaasay,
Nirkaamang bibhootay, samastul saroopay,
Kukarmang pranaasi; su dharmang bibhootay. 197
Sada Sachidaanand satrang pranaasee.
Karimul kuninda samastul nivaasee.
Ajaib bibhootay gajaib ganimay,
Hariang Kariang Karimul rahimay. 198
Chatr chakr vartee chatr chakr bhugtay,
Suyambhav subhang sarabdaa sarab jugtay,
Dukaalang pranaase dyaalang saroopay
Sadaa ang sangay abhangang bibhootay. 199 (10)

4. JAAP

Bhujang Prayaat Chhand

I bow to the Honourable Lord; I bow to the All-Destroyer.
You are beyond treasure and name, You pervade in all places.
You are desireless in Your glory and present in everything.
You are the Destroyer of sins; Your righteous
Law¹ controls everything. (197)
You are truth and Bliss and the Scourge of enemies,
The Bestower of blessings who resides in every being.
Your glory is wonderful; You are the Destroyer of tyrants.
You can annihilate and create; You are benevolent and compassionate.(198)
You pervade in all directions, You enjoy the things of the universe.
You are self-illumined, beautiful and present in all beings.
You are the Destroyer of the pain of birth and death and you are the personification of compassion.
You are ever present within us. Your Essence is indestructible (199) (10)

---

1. The Divine Law or **Hukam** controls all creation.

5. ਅਕਾਲ ਉਸਤਤਿ ਪਾਤਿਸ਼ਾਹੀ ੧੦ ॥

ਅਕਾਲ ਪੁਰਖ ਕੀ ਰੱਛਾ ਹਮ ਨੈ। ਸਰਬ ਲੋਹ ਕੀ ਰੱਛਿਆ ਹਮ ਨੈ।
ਸਰਬਕਾਲ ਜੀ ਕੀ ਰੱਛਿਆ ਹਮ ਨੈ।
ਸਰਬ ਲੋਹ ਜੀ ਦੀ ਸਦਾ ਰੱਛਿਆ ਹਮ ਨੈ ॥੧॥

ਤ੍ਵ ਪ੍ਰਸਾਦਿ ॥ ਚੌਪਈ ॥

ਪ੍ਰਣਵੋ ਆਦਿ ਏਕੰਕਾਰਾ। ਜਲ ਥਲ ਮਹੀਅਲ ਕੀਓ ਪਸਾਰਾ।
ਆਦਿ ਪੁਰਖ ਅਬਗਤਿ ਅਬਿਨਾਸੀ। ਲੋਕ ਚਤੁ ਦਸਿ ਜੋਤਿ ਪ੍ਰਕਾਸੀ ॥੧॥
ਹਸਤਿ ਕੀਟ ਕੇ ਬੀਚ ਸਮਾਨਾ। ਰਾਵ ਰੰਕ ਜਿਹ ਇਕਸਰ ਜਾਨਾ।
ਅਦ੍ਵੈ ਅਲਖ ਪੁਰਖ ਅਬਿਗਾਮੀ। ਸਭ ਘਟ ਘਟ ਕੇ ਅੰਤਰਜਾਮੀ ॥੨॥

5. Akaal Ustat Patshaahi Dasvee

Akaal purakh kee rachhaa hum nai,
Sarab loh kee rachhaa hum nai,
Sarab kaal ji ki rachhia hum nai
Sarab loh ji di sadaa rachhia hum nai

Tav Parsaad Chaupai

Pranavo aad ekankaaraa,
Jal thal maheeal keo pasaaraa,
Aad purakh abgat abnaasi,
Lok chatra das jot prakaasi. 1
Hast keet kay beech samaanaa
Raav runk jah iksar jaanaa.
Advai alakh purakh abgaamee
Sabh ghat ghat kay antarjaamee. 2

5. Akal Ustat Patshahi Dasvee.

My only Refuge is my God, the Timeless Being.
Who is All-steel, All-death, All-power,
May He protect me !

Tav Prasaad Chaupai

I bow to the Primal God,
Who pervades the earth, the waters and the interspace.
The First Person, Absolute and Deathless,
Whose light is manifest in the fourteen spheres. 1

He is as much in the elephant as in the ant.
He looks upon the rich and the poor alike.
Unique, Unknowable, not torn by Doubt,
And the Inner-knower of all hearts is He. 2

6. ਅਕਾਲ ਉਸਤਤਿ ॥ ਤ੍ਵ ਪ੍ਰਸਾਦਿ ॥ ਲਘੁਨਰਾਜ ਛੰਦ

ਜਲੇ ਹਰੀ । ਥਲੇ ਹਰੀ । ਉਰੇ ਹਰੀ । ਬਨੇ ਹਰੀ ॥੫੧॥
ਗਿਰੇ ਹਰੀ । ਗੁਫੇ ਹਰੀ । ਛਿਤੇ ਹਰੀ । ਨਭੇ ਹਰੀ ॥੫੨॥
ਈਹਾਂ ਹਰੀ । ਊਹਾਂ ਹਰੀ । ਜ਼ਿਮੀ ਹਰੀ । ਜਮਾਂ ਹਰੀ ॥੫੩॥
ਅਲੇਖ ਹਰੀ । ਅਭੇਖ ਹਰੀ । ਅਦੋਖ ਹਰੀ । ਅਦ੍ਵੈਖ ਹਰੀ ॥੫੪॥
ਅਕਾਲ ਹਰੀ । ਅਪਾਲ ਹਰੀ । ਅਛੇਦ ਹਰੀ । ਅਭੇਦ ਹਰੀ ॥੫੫॥
ਅਜੰਤ੍ਰ ਹਰੀ । ਅਮੰਤ੍ਰ ਹਰੀ । ਸੁਤੇਜ ਹਰੀ । ਅਤੰਤ੍ਰ ਹਰੀ ॥੫੬॥

6. Akaal Ustat Tav Prasaad, Laghunraj Chhand

Jalay Hari, thhalay Hari; Uray Hari, banay Hari ; 51
Giray Hari, Gufay Hari ; Chhitay Hari, nabhay Hari ; 52
Eehaa Hari, Oohaa Hari ; Zimee Hari, zamaa Hari ; 53
Alekh Hari, Abhekh Hari ; Adokh Hari, adwekh Hari ; 54
Akaal Hari, apaal Hari ; Achhed Hari, Abhed Hari ; 55
Ajantra Hari, Amantra Hari ; Sutej Hari, Atantra Hari ; 56.

6. Akaal Ustat Tav Prasaad Laghunraj Chhand

God is in the waters and upon the earth,
In the heart as in the forest.51

Over the high mountains as in the deep caves,
Across the skies, as upon land. 52

Here, as well as there,
In the world, as in the yond. 53

Unaccountable and without a garb,
    Not subject to pain,
        and the enemy of no one ! 54

Above Time. Unsustained (by another),
Unpierceable and Mysterious. 55

Not attained through charms, or verbal formulas or diagrams.[1]
    He is the Most Magnificent Splendour. 56

---

1. Religious magicians apply these tricks to rob the gullible.

7. ਤੁ ਪ੍ਰਸਾਦਿ ਸਵੱਯੇ ॥

(ਅਕਾਲ ਉਸਤਤਿ)

ਦੀਨਨ ਕੀ ਪ੍ਰਤਿਪਾਲ ਕਰੈ ਨਿਤ ਸੰਤ ਉਬਾਰ ਗਨੀਮਨ ਗਾਰੈ ॥
ਪੱਛ ਪਸੂ ਨਗ ਨਾਗ ਨਰਾਧਿਪ ਸਰਬ ਸਮੈ ਸਭ ਕੋ ਪ੍ਰਤਿਪਾਰੈ ।
ਪੋਖਤ ਹੈ ਜਲ ਮੈ ਥਲ ਮੈ ਪਲ ਮੈ ਕਲ ਕੇ ਨਹੀ ਕਰਮ ਬਿਚਾਰੈ ॥
ਦੀਨ ਦਇਆਲ ਦਇਆ ਨਿਧਿ ਦੋਖਨ ਦੇਖਤ ਹੈ ਪਰ ਦੇਤ ਨ ਹਾਰੈ ॥੧॥੨੪੩॥

7. Tav Prasaad Savaiye (Akaal Ustat)

Dinan kee pritpaal karay nit sant ubaar ganeeman gaaray.

Pachh pasoo nug naag naradhip sarab samay subh ko pritpaaray.

Pokhat hai jal mai thal mai pal mai kal kay nahi karam beechaaray.

Din dayal daya nidh dokhan dekhat hai pur det na haaray. 1   (34)

7. Tav Prasaad Savaiye (Akaal Ustat)

God always looks after the weak, destroys foes and protects the saints.

God at all times takes care of all including birds, beasts, mountains, snakes and kings.

God cherishes all living beings in the sea and on the land and does not reflect on their evil deeds.

God is benevolent to the poor and is an ocean of compassion;

He sees the sins of the recipients, but does not cease bestowing gifts on them. (34)

8. ਅਕਾਲ ਉਸਤਤਿ ॥

ਕੇਤੇ ਇੰਦ੍ਰ ਦੁਆਰ ਕੇਤੇ ਬ੍ਰਹਮਾ ਮੁਖਚਾਰ,
ਕੇਤੇ ਕ੍ਰਿਸ਼ਨਾ ਅਵਤਾਰ, ਕੇਤੇ ਰਾਮ ਕਹੀਅਤੁ ਹੈ।
ਕੇਤੇ ਸਸਿ ਰਾਸੀ, ਕੇਤੇ ਸੂਰਜ ਪ੍ਰਕਾਸੀ:
ਕੇਤੇ ਮੁੰਡੀਆ ਉਦਾਸੀ, ਜੋਗ ਦੁਆਰਿ ਦਹੀਅਤੁ ਹੈ।
ਕੇਤੇ ਮਹਾਂਦੀਨ ਕੇਤੇ ਬਿਆਸ ਸੇ ਪ੍ਰਬੀਨ,
ਕੇਤੇ ਕੁਮੇਰਾਂ ਕੁਲੀਨ, ਕੇਤੇ ਜੱਛ ਕਹੀਅਤੁ ਹੈ।
ਕਰਤੇ ਹੈਂ ਬਿਚਾਰ, ਪੈ ਨ ਪੂਰਨ ਕੋ ਪਾਵੈ ਪਾਰ,
ਤਾਂ ਹੀ ਤੇ ਅਪਾਰ, ਨਿਰਾਧਾਰ ਲਹੀਅਤੁ ਹੈ॥੨੫੭॥

8. Akaal Ustat

Ketay Indra duar, ketay Brahmaa mukhchaar,
Ketay Krishnaa avtaar, Ketay Raam kaheeat hai,
Ketay sas raasi, ketlay sooraj prakaasi,
Ketay mundeeaa udaasee, jog duar daheeat hai,
Ketay mahaadeen, ketay Biaas say prabeen.
Ketay kumer kuleen, ketay jachh kaheeat hai.
Kartay hain bichaar, pai na pooran ko pavai paar.
Taa hee tay apaar, niraadhaar laheeat hai. 257.

8. Akaal Ustat

There are countless Indras at Your door, and countless
four-faced Brahmas, and Krishnas and Ramas.
And those claiming kinship with the moon and the sun,
and the close-cropped sanyasis, and the yogis too bow down to You.
And many were the Mohammads, and the clever ones
like Vyasa[1], and Kuberas of clean descent, and so many Yakshas.
They all think of You but, O Perfect One, they know
not end : that is how You are called
Infinite and the Self-sufficient Being 257

---

1. The reciter of Vedas.

9. ਅਕਾਲ ਉਸਤਤਿ

ਫਾਰਸੀ ਫਿਰੰਗੀ, ਫਰਾਂਸੀਸ ਕੇ ਦੁਰੰਗੀ,
'ਮਕਰਾਨ' ਕੇ ਮ੍ਰਿਦੰਗੀ ਤੇਰੇ ਗੀਤ ਗਾਈਅਤੁ ਹੈ।
ਭੱਖਰੀ ਕੰਧਾਰੀ, ਗੋਰਿ ਗੱਖਰੀ ਗਰਦੇਜਾਚਾਰੀ,
ਪਉਨ ਕੇ ਅਹਾਰੀ, ਤੇਰੇ ਨਾਮੁ ਧਿਆਈਅਤੁ ਹੈਂ।
ਪੂਰਬ 'ਪਲਾਊ" ਕਾਮਰੂਪ 'ਅਉ ਕਮਾਊ":
ਸਰਬ ਠਉਰ ਮੈ ਬਿਰਾਜੈ, ਜਹਾਂ ਜਹਾਂ ਜਾਈਅਤੁ ਹੈ।
ਪੂਰਨ ਪ੍ਰਤਾਪੀ, ਜੰਤ੍ਰ ਮੰਤ੍ਰ ਤੇ ਅਤਾਪੀ ਨਾਥ।
ਕੀਰਤਿ ਤਿਹਾਰੀ ਕੋ ਨ ਪਾਰ ਪਾਈਅਤੁ ਹੈ।।੨੬੬।।

9. Akaal Ustat

Faarsee firangee, fransis kay durangee,
Makraan kay mirdangee teray geet gaaeeat hai.
Bhakhree kandhaaree gor gakhree gardejaachaari ;
Paun kay ahaari, teray naam dhiaaeeat hai
Poorb palaaoo, kaamroop au kamaaoo,
Sabh thhaur mai biraajai, jahaa jahaa jaaeat hai.
Pooran partaapee, jantra mantra kay ataape naath,
Keerat tihaaree ko, na paar paaeeat hai. 266.

9. Akal Ustat

O God, everyone dwells upon You– the Persians,
    the Ferangis and the colourful men of France,
And, the delicate people of Makran too hymn Your Praise,
And the dwellers of Bhakhar, of Kandhar and Ghaur,
    and the Gakhars, and the Gurdezis too, and fasting men who live only on air.
In the east in Palau, in Kamrup and in Kamaun, wherever
    one goes, one finds You Supreme.
Of Perfect Glory, whom incantations can charm not,
    O Lord, there is no limit to Your laudation. (266)

10. ਤ੍ਵ ਪ੍ਰਸਾਦਿ ਸਵੱਯੇ ॥

ਕਾਮ ਨ ਕ੍ਰੋਧ ਨ ਲੋਭ ਨ ਮੋਹ ਨ ਰੋਗ ਨ ਸੋਗ ਨ ਭੋਗ ਨ ਭੈ ਹੈ ॥
ਦੇਹ ਬਿਹੀਨ ਸਨੇਹ ਸਭੋ ਤਨ ਨੇਹ ਬਿਰਕਤ ਅਗੇਹ ਅਛੈ ਹੈ ॥
ਜਾਨ ਕੋ ਦੇਤ ਅਜਾਨ ਕੋ ਦੇਤ ਜਮੀਨ ਕੋ ਦੇਤ ਜਮਾਨ ਕੋ ਦੈ ਹੈ ॥
ਕਾਹੇ ਕੋ ਡੋਲਤ ਹੈ ਤੁਮਰੀ ਸੁਧ ਸੁੰਦਰ ਸ੍ਰੀ ਪਦਮਾਪਤਿ ਲੈ ਹੈ ॥੫॥੨੪੭॥

10. Tav Prasaad Savaiye

Kaam na Krodh na lobh na moh na rog na sog na bhog ba bhai hai.

Deh biheen saneh sabho tun neh birkat ageh achhai hai.

Jaan ko det ajaan ko det jameen ko det jamaan ko dai hai.

Kahay ko dolat hai tumri sudh sundar Sri Padmapat lai hai. 5. 247 (35)

10. Tav Prasaad Savaiye

God is not subject to lust, anger, greed, worldly attachement, disease, sorrow, enjoyment or fear.

God has no body; He has love for all, yet He has no sensual feeling; He has no home and is beyond destruction.

God gives to those who are learned and to those who are ignorant; He gives to all beings of the earth and heaven.

O man, Why do you feel worried, when the Supreme and Beautiful Lord is to take care of you ? (35)

11. ਤੂ ਪ੍ਰਸਾਦਿ ਸਵੱਯੇ ॥

ਰੋਗਨ ਤੇ ਅਰ ਸੋਗਨ ਤੇ ਜਲ ਜੋਗਨ ਤੇ ਬਹੁ ਭਾਂਤਿ ਬਚਾਵੈ ॥
ਸੱਤ੍ਰੁ ਅਨੇਕ ਚਲਾਵਤ ਘਾਵ ਤਊ ਤਨ ਏਕ ਨ ਲਾਗਨ ਪਾਵੈ ॥
ਰਾਖਤ ਹੈ ਅਪਨੋ ਕਰ ਦੈਕਰ ਪਾਪ ਸੰਬੂਹ ਨ ਭੇਟਨ ਪਾਵੈ ॥
ਔਰ ਕੀ ਬਾਤ ਕਹਾ ਕਹ ਤੋਸੋ ਸੁ ਪੇਟ ਹੀ ਕੇ ਪਟ ਬੀਚ ਬਚਾਵੈ ॥੬॥੨੪੮॥

11. Tav Prasaad Savaiye

Rogan tay ar sogan tay jal jogan tay bah bhant bachaavai,

Satr anek chalavat ghav tau tan ek na lagan paavai.

Rakhat hai apno kar dekar paap sambooh na bhetan paavai.

Aur ki baat kahaa kah to sau su pet hee kay pat beech bachaavai. 6.
248 (35)

11. Tav Prasaad Savaiye

God saves people in different ways from diseases, sorrows and water-animals.

Our foes may direct their blows at us and yet none of them can scrape our bodies.

God protects us with His hands and prevents the army of sinners from harming us.

Why do we talk of anything else ? God protects the individual even inside the womb. (35)

12. ਤ੍ਵ ਪ੍ਰਸਾਦਿ ਸਵੱਯੇ ॥

ਨਾਰਦ ਸੇ ਚਤੁਰਾਨਨ ਸੇ ਰੁਮਨਾਰਿਖ ਸੇ ਸਭਹੂੰ ਮਿਲਿ ਗਾਇਓ ॥
ਬੇਦ ਕਤੇਬ ਨ ਭੇਦ ਲਖਿਓ ਸਭ ਹਾਰ ਪਰੇ ਹਰਿ ਹਾਥ ਨ ਆਇਓ ॥
ਪਾਇ ਸਕੈ ਨਹੀ ਪਾਰ ਉਮਾਪਤਿ ਸਿੱਧ ਸਨਾਥ ਸਨੰਤਨ ਧਿਆਇਓ ॥
ਧਿਆਨ ਧਰੋ ਤਿਹ ਕੋ ਮਨ ਮੈਂ ਜਿਹ ਕੋ ਅਮਿਤੋਜ ਸਭੈ ਜਗ ਛਾਇਓ ॥੮॥੨੫੦॥

12. Tav Prasaad Savaiye

Naarad say chaturaanan say rumnaarikh say sabhahoo mil gaaio,

Bed Kateb na bhed lakhiyo sabh haar paray Har haath na aaio,

Pai sakay nahi paar Umaapat sidh sanaath sanantan dhiaaio,

Dhian dharo teh ko man mai jih ko amitoj sabhai jag chhaaio.

8.250 (35)

12. Tav Prasaad Savaiye

All living beings like Narad,[1] Brahma[2] Rumna[3] and others join together in singing the glory of God.

Vedas and Katebas (Semitic scriptures) have not unravelled God's mystery; they have been wearied in their search, but have not been able to attain to Him.

Shiva, the spouse of Uma, has not been able to discover the limits of God's glory; Siddhas,[4] mystics and the sons of Brahma meditate on the Lord.

O man, meditate sincerely in your heart on God, whose limitless power pervades the entire universe (35)

---

1. **Narad :** The name of an Indian saint said to be the author of Bhakti Sutra.
2. **Brahma :** The first of the Hindu Trinity known as the Creator.
3. **Rumna :** An Indian saint, also called Lomahrakhan, was a disciple of saint Vyas.
4. **Siddhas :** Yogis possessing occult powers.

13. ਤ੍ਰਿਭੰਗੀ ਛੰਦ (ਬਚਿਤ੍ਰ ਨਾਟਕ)

ਖਗ ਖੰਡ ਬਿਹੰਡੰ, ਖਲ ਦਲ ਖੰਡੰ, ਅਤਿ ਰਣ ਮੰਡੰ, ਬਰਬੰਡੰ ॥
ਭੁਜਦੰਡ ਅਖੰਡੰ, ਤੇਜ ਪ੍ਰਚੰਡੰ, ਜੋਤਿ ਅਮੰਡੰ, ਭਾਨ ਪ੍ਰਭੰ ॥
ਸੁਖ ਸੰਤਾ ਕਰਣੰ, ਦੁਰਮਤਿ ਦਰਣੰ, ਕਿਲਬਿਖ ਹਰਣੰ, ਅਸ ਸਰਣੰ ॥
ਜੈ ਜੈ ਜਗ ਕਾਰਣ, ਸ੍ਰਿਸਟਿ ਉਬਾਰਣ, ਮਮ ਪ੍ਰਤਿਪਾਰਣ ਜੈ ਤੇਗੰ ॥੨॥

13. Tribhangi Chhand (Bachitar Natak)

Khag khand bihandang, khal dal khandang, ut run mandang, barbandang,
Bhujdand akhandang, tej prachandang, jot amandang, bhan prabhang,
Sukh santa karnang, durmat darnang, kilbikh harnang, us sarnang,
Jai jai jug karan, srisht ubaran, mum pritpaaran jai teghang. 2 (39)

13. Tribhangi Chhand (Bachitar Natak)

You[1] (the Sword) are the conqueror of countries and the destroyer of the armies of the wicked on the battle field; you are the fittest decoration of warriors.

Your arm is irresistible, your brightness is resplendent and your radiance and aura dazzle like the sun.

You bring happiness to the saintly and frighten the wicked and scatter the sinners; I seek your shelter.

Hail ! Hail ! to the Creator, the Sustainer of the universe;

Hail to the Holy Sword, the Protector of creation (39)

---

1. God as the embodiment of power is represented by the Sword. He is the Destroyer of the wicked and is therefore identified with the Sword or 'Bhagwati'.

14. ਸਵੈਯਾ ॥

ਪਾਂਇ ਗਹੇ ਜਬਤੇ ਤੁਮਰੇ ਤਬਤੇ ਕੋਊ ਆਂਖ ਤਰੇ ਨਹੀ ਆਨਯੋ ॥

ਰਾਮ ਰਹੀਮ ਪੁਰਾਨ ਕੁਰਾਨ ਅਨੇਕ ਕਹੈਂ ਮਤ ਏਕ ਨ ਮਾਨਯੋ ॥

ਸਿਮ੍ਰਿਤਿ ਸਾਸਤ੍ਰ ਬੇਦ ਸਬੈ ਬਹੁ ਭੇਦ ਕਹੈਂ ਹਮ ਏਕ ਨ ਜਾਨਯੋ ॥

ਸ੍ਰੀ ਅਸਿਪਾਨ ਕ੍ਰਿਪਾ ਤੁਮਰੀ ਕਰ ਮੈਂ ਨ ਕਹਯੋ ਸਭ ਤੋਹਿ ਬਖਾਨਯੋ ॥੧॥

14. Savaiya

Pah gahay jabtay tumray tab tay kou ankh taray nahi aanyo.

Ram Rahim Puran Qoran anek kahay mut ek na maanyo.

Simrat Shastra Bed sabai bahu bhed kahai hum ek na jaanyo.

Sri Aspaan kripa tumri kar mai na kahyo Sabh toh bakhaanyo. 1.

(254)

14. Savaiya (Ram Avtar)

Ever since I have grasped God's feet, I have not thought of anybody else.

I do not accept the doctrines enunciated by various faiths, believing in Ram, Rahim, Puranas[1] and Qoran.

The Simritis,[2] Shastras[3] and the Vedas[4] mention different concepts but I do not subscribe to any of them.

O God, the Sword-bearer (of justice)! With Your Grace, all that has been uttered by me has been done under Your command. (254)

---

1. **Puranas** : The ancient Hindu books of legend and mythology.
2. **Simritis** : Traditional law-books of the Hindus.
3. **Shastras** : The six books of Indian philosophy.
4. **Vedas** : The four scriptures of the Hindus.

15. ਰਾਗੁ ਸੋਰਠਿ ॥

ਪ੍ਰਭ ਜੂ ਤੋ ਕਹਿ ਲਾਜ ਹਮਾਰੀ ॥
ਨੀਲ ਕੰਠ ਨਰ ਹਰਿ ਨਾਰਾਇਣ ਨੀਲ ਬਸਨ ਬਨਵਾਰੀ ॥੧॥ ਰਹਾਉ ॥
ਪਰਮ ਪੁਰਖ ਪਰਮੇਸੁਰ ਸੁਆਮੀ ਪਾਵਨ ਪਉਨ ਅਹਾਰੀ ॥
ਮਾਧਵ ਮਹਾ ਜੋਤ ਮਧੁ ਮਰਦਨ ਮਾਨ ਮੁਕੰਦ ਮੁਰਾਰੀ ॥੧॥
ਨਿਰਬਿਕਾਰ ਨਿਰਜੁਰ ਨਿੰਦ੍ਰਾ ਬਿਨ ਨਿਰਬਿਖ ਨਰਕ ਨਿਵਾਰੀ ॥
ਕ੍ਰਿਪਾ ਸਿੰਧ ਕਾਲ ਤ੍ਰੈ ਦਰਸੀ ਕੁਕ੍ਰਿਤ ਪ੍ਰਨਾਸਨ ਕਾਰੀ ॥੨॥
ਧਨੁਰ ਪਾਨ ਧ੍ਰਿਤ ਮਾਨ ਧਰਾਧਰ ਅਨ ਬਿਕਾਰ ਅਸਿ ਧਾਰੀ ॥
ਹੌਂ ਮਤਿ ਮੰਦ ਚਰਨ ਸਰਨਾਗਤਿ ਕਰਿ ਗਹਿ ਲੇਹੁ ਉਬਾਰੀ ॥੩॥੧॥

15. Raag Sorath

Prabh joo to kah laaj hamari.

Neel kanthh narhar Narain neel basan banwaari. 1. Rahau

Param Purkh Parmeswar Swaami paavan paun ahaari.

Madhav maha jot madh mardan maan mukand muraari. 1.

Nirbikaar nir jur nindraa bin nirbikh narak nivaari.

Kirpa sindh kaal trai darsi kukrit parnasan kaari. 2

Dhanurpaan dhrit maan dharadhar unbikar asdhaari.

Hau mat mand charan sarnaagat kar gah leh ubaari. 3   (710)

15. Raag Sorath (Shabad Hazare)

O God! My repute (honour) is in Your hands.

You can save me by taking the form of the blue-throated Shiva or the Man-lion or Vishnu. You move in the water (like Balram) and dwell in the forest (like Krishna). Pause.

You are the Primal Being, the Supreme Lord, the Sanctifying Being living on air.

You are the Lord of Lakshmi (goddes of wealth) and the great Light, Vishnu the destroyer of demon Madhu's pride[1], and Krishna the killer of demon Mur.

You are sinless and not subject to decline. You are not subject to sleep and evil inclinations.

You save people from hell.

You are Ocean of Compassion. You are Omniscent in all ages and the Destroyer of evil actions.

You carry a bow in Your hands. You are also patient. You are the support of the earth, faultless and the Wielder of the sword.

I, who am foolish, have taken refuge at Your feet. Do grab my hand and save me. (710)

---

1. **Vishun** is called Madhusudan—the killer of Madhu.

16. ਰਾਗੁ ਕਲਿਆਨ ॥

ਬਿਨ ਕਰਤਾਰ ਨ ਕਿਰਤਮ ਮਾਨੋ ॥

ਆਦਿ ਅਜੋਨਿ ਅਜੈ ਅਬਿਨਾਸੀ ਤਿਹ ਪਰਮੇਸਰ ਜਾਨੋ ॥੧॥ ਰਹਾਉ ॥

ਕਹਾ ਭਯੋ ਜੋ ਆਨਿ ਜਗਤ ਮੈ ਦਸਕ ਅਸੁਰ ਹਰਿ ਘਾਏ ।

ਅਧਿਕ ਪ੍ਰਪੰਚ ਦਿਖਾਇ ਸਭਨ ਕਹ ਆਪਹਿ ਬ੍ਰਹਮੁ ਕਹਾਏ ॥੧॥

ਭੰਜਨ ਗੜ੍ਹਨ ਸਮਰਥ ਸਦਾ ਪ੍ਰਭ ਸੋ ਕਿਮ ਜਾਤ ਗਿਨਾਯੋ ॥

ਤਾਂ ਤੇ ਸਰਬ ਕਾਲ ਕੇ ਅਸਿ ਕੋ ਘਾਇ ਬਚਾਇ ਨ ਆਯੋ ॥੨॥

ਕੈਸੇ ਤੋਹਿ ਤਾਰਿ ਹੈ ਸੁਨਿ ਜੜ ਆਪ ਡੁਬਯੋ ਭਵ ਸਾਗਰ ॥

ਛੁਟਿਹੋ ਕਾਲ ਫਾਸ ਤੇ ਤਬਹੀ ਗਹੋ ਸਰਨਿ ਜਗਤਾਗਰ ॥੩॥੧॥

16. Raag Kaliaan

Bin Kartaar na kirtam maano.

Aad ajon ajai abnasi teh Parmesar jaano. 1. Rahau

Kahaa bhaio jo aan jagat mai dasak asur har ghaae.

Adhak parpanch dikhaae sabhan kah apeh Braham kahaae. 1.

Bhanjan garhan samrath sadaa Prabh so kim jaat ginaayo.

Tante sarab kaal ke as ko ghai bachai na aayo 2.

Kaisay toh taar hai sun jar aap dubiyo bhavsaagar.

Chhutyo kaal faas te tabhi gaho saran jagtaagar. 3. 1 (710)

16. Raag Kaliaan [Kalyan] (Shabad Hazare)

O man, do not worship anything other than the Creator.

Regard God, who was from the beginning Unborn, Invincible and Indestructible as the Supreme Being. Pause.

What did it matter if Vishnu[1] came into the world and killed the demons?

By showing his wiles to people, he exhorted them to call him God.

How can he (Vishnu) be called God, the Destroyer, the Creator, the Omnipotent and the Eternal!

He (Vishnu) could not save himself from the blow of the sword of Death.

O stupid person, listen, how can he, who himself is sunk in the ocean of the world, save you?

You can escape from the noose of Death, only if you seek the refuge of the One who existed before the world came into being. (710)

---

1. **Vishnu**: The second of the Hindu Trinity, known as the Sustainer or Preserver.

17. ਤਿਲੰਗ ਕਾਫੀ ॥

ਕੇਵਲ ਕਾਲਈ ਕਰਤਾਰ ॥
ਆਦਿ ਅੰਤ ਅਨੰਤਿ ਮੂਰਤ ਗੜ੍ਹਨ ਭੰਜਨਹਾਰ ॥੧॥ ਰਹਾਉ ॥
ਨਿੰਦ ਉਸਤਤ ਜਉਨ ਕੇ ਸਮ ਸਤ੍ਰੁ ਮਿਤ੍ਰ ਨਾ ਕੋਇ ॥
ਕਉਨ ਬਾਟ ਪਰੀ ਤਿਸੈ ਪਥ ਸਾਰਥੀ ਰਥ ਹੋਇ ॥੧॥
ਤਾਤ ਮਾਤ ਨ ਜਾਤ ਜਾਕਰ ਪੁਤ੍ਰ ਪੋਤ੍ਰ ਮੁਕੰਦ ॥
ਕਉਨ ਕਾਜ ਕਹਾਹਿੰਗੋ ਆਨਿ ਦੇਵਕਿ ਨੰਦ ॥੨॥
ਦੇਵ ਦੈਤ ਦਿਸਾ ਵਿਸਾ ਜਿਹ ਕੀਨ ਸਰਬ ਪਸਾਰ ॥
ਕਉਨ ਉਪਮਾ ਤਉਨ ਕੋ ਮੁਖ ਲੇਤ ਨਾਮੁ ਮੁਰਾਰ ॥੩॥੧॥

17. Tilang Kafi

Kewal kaalaee Kartar.

Aad ant anant moorat garhan bhanjanhaar. 1. Rahau

Nind ustat jaun kay sam satra mitra na koi.

Kaun baat pari tisai path sarthi rath hoi 1.

Taat maat na jaat jaakar putr potra mukand.

Kaun kaaj kahahingay aan Devki nand. 2.

Dev dait disaa visaa jeh keen sarab pasaar.

Kaun upmaa taun ko mukh let nam Muraar 3. 1.   (711)

17. Tilang Kafi (Shabad Hazare)

God is the sole Creator.

God is the beginning and the end of everything. He is the Creator and Destroyer. Pause.

For God, praise or censure is equal ; He has no friend or foe.

What need had he to be the driver of (Arjan's) chariot ?[1]

God, the Bestower of salvation, has neither father nor mother, nor caste nor son nor grandson.

What for should he have to come into the world to be known as the son of Devki ?[2]

He has created gods and demons and pervades in all directions.

What glory do we offer Him when we call Him by the name of Murar ?[3]

(711)

---

1. **Lord Krishna** was the Charioteer of Arjan's chariot during the War of Mahabharata. As such he cannot be called God.
2. **Lord Krishna,** the son of Devki, is regarded as an incarnation of God by the Hindus. God is not subject to death and Lord Krishna cannot be called God.
3. **Lord Krishna** is called Murar/Murari because he killed the demon known as Mur.

18. ਰਾਗੁ ਬਿਲਾਵਲ ॥

ਸੋ ਕਿਸ ਮਾਨਸ ਰੂਪ ਕਹਾਏ ॥
ਸਿੱਧ ਸਮਾਧ ਸਾਧ ਕਰ ਹਾਰੇ ਕਜੇ ਹੂੰ ਨ ਦੇਖਨ ਪਾਏ ॥੧॥ ਰਹਾਉ ॥
ਨਾਰਦ ਬਿਆਸ ਪਰਾਸਰ ਧ੍ਰੂ ਸੋ ਧਿਆਵਤ ਧਿਆਨ ਲਗਾਏ ॥
ਬੇਦ ਪੁਰਾਨ ਹਾਰ ਹਠ ਛਾਡਿਓ ਤੱਦਪਿ ਧਿਆਨ ਨ ਆਏ ॥੧॥
ਦਾਨਵ ਦੇਵ ਪਿਸਾਚ ਪ੍ਰੇਤ ਤੇ ਨੇਤਹਿ ਨੇਤਿ ਕਹਾਏ ॥
ਸੂਛਮ ਤੇ ਸੂਛਮ ਕਰ ਚੀਨੇ ਬ੍ਰਿੱਧਨ ਬ੍ਰਿੱਧ ਬਤਾਏ ॥੨॥
ਭੂਮਿ ਅਕਾਸ ਪਾਤਾਲ ਸਬੈ ਸਜਿ ਏਕ ਅਨੇਕ ਸਦਾਏ ॥
ਸੋ ਨਰ ਕਾਲ ਫਾਸ ਤੇ ਬਾਚੇ ਜੋ ਹਰਿ ਸਰਨ ਸਿਧਾਏ ॥੩॥੧॥

18. Raag Bilaaval

So kim maanas roop kahaay.

Sidh samaadh sadh kar haaray kayo hoo na dekhan paay. 1. Rahau

Narad Biyas Praasar Dhru say dhiavat dhian lagaay.

Bed puran haar hath chhadiyo tadap dhian na aay. 1

Daanav dev pisaach pret tay netah net kahaay.

Soochham tay soochham kar cheenay bridhan bridh bataay 2.

Bhoom akaas pataal sabhai saj ek anek sadaay.

So nar kaal faas tay baachay jo Har saran sidhaay. 3 1.

(711)

18. Raag Bilaaval (Shabad Hazare)

Why should God appear in human form ?

Siddhas have failed to find Him anywhere, inspite of their meditations. Pause.

Narad,[1] Bias[2], Prasur[3], Dhru[4] have sincerely meditated on God.

The Vedas and the Puranas failed and hence gave up all their efforts for realising Him.

Demons, gods, fiends and goblins say that God is infinite.

God has been represented as the smallest of the small and the biggest of the big.

God created earth, heaven and all the nether regions and though He is one, He is known as "The Many".

So the person who seeks refuge in God's protection will escape the noose of Death. (711)

---

1. **Narad** : An ancient Indian sage.
2. **Bias** : An ancient Indian sage, also called Vyas.
3. **Prasur** : An ancient Indian saint.
4. **Dhru** : An ancient Indian child-saint. It is said that on account of his bhakti, he was raised to the position of the polar star.

19. ਰਾਗੁ ਦੇਵਗੰਧਾਰੀ ॥

ਇਕ ਬਿਨ ਦੂਸਰ ਸੋ ਨ ਚਿਨਾਰ ॥
ਭੰਜਨ ਗੜ੍ਹਨ ਸਮਰਥ ਸਦਾ ਪ੍ਰਭ ਜਾਨਤ ਹੈ ਕਰਤਾਰ ॥੧॥ ਰਹਾਉ ॥
ਕਹਾ ਭਇਓ ਜੋ ਅਤਿ ਹਿਤ ਚਿਤ ਕਰ ਬਹੁ ਬਿਧਿ ਸਿਲਾ ਪੁਜਾਈ ॥
ਪ੍ਰਾਨ ਥਕਿਓ ਪਾਹਿਨ ਕਹਿ ਪਰਸਤ ਕਛੁ ਕਰ ਸਿੱਧ ਨ ਆਈ ॥੧॥
ਅੱਛਤ ਧੂਪ ਦੀਪ ਅਰਪਤ ਹੈ ਪਾਹਨ ਕਛੁ ਨ ਖੈ ਹੈ ॥
ਤਾਂ ਮੈ ਕਹਾਂ ਸਿੱਧ ਹੈ ਰੇ ਜੜ ਤੋਹਿ ਕਛੁ ਬਰ ਦੈ ਹੈ ॥੨॥
ਜੋ ਜੀਜ ਹੋਤ ਦੇਤ ਕਛੁ ਤੁਹਿ ਕਰ ਮਨ ਬਚ ਕਰਮ ਬਿਚਾਰ ॥
ਕੇਵਲ ਏਕ ਸਰਣ ਸੁਆਮੀ ਬਿਨ ਯੋ ਨਹਿ ਕਤਹਿ ਉਧਾਰ ॥੩॥੧॥

19. Raag Devagandhari

Ik bin doosar so na chinaar,

Bhanjan garhan samrath sadaa Prabh jaanat hai Kartar. 1. Rahau

Kahaa bhaio jo at hit chit kar bahu bidh silaa pujaee.

Praan thakio paahan kah parsat kachu kar sidh na aee. 1.

Achhat dhoop deep arpat hai, paahan kachhoo na khai hai.

Ta mai kaha sidh hai ray jar toh kachhu bar dai hai. 2.

Jo jeea hot det kachh tuh kar man bach karam bichaar.

Kewal ek saran suaami bin yo nah katah udhaar. 3.1. (711)

19. Raag Devagandhari (Shabad Hazare)

Except one God, do not accept anyone else.

God is the Destroyer, the Designer, the Omnipotent and the Eternal, who is known as the Creator. Pause.

Of what value is the worship of stones[1] in different ways, done with great zeal?

Life is spent in worshipping stones without any spiritual achievement.

Rice, incense and oil-torches are offered to stones, but they are lifeless.

O dullard! What spiritual potential is in stones? What can they give you?

If these stones had any life, they could have given you something in your thoughts, words and deeds.

There is no spiritiual fulfilment, except through seeking the refuge of the One Lord. (711)

---

1. Various forms of Hindu worship of idols are not approved by Guru Gobind Singh.

20. ਸਵੱਯੇ ॥

ਜੋਂ ਕਹੋ ਰਾਮ ਅਜੋਨ ਅਜੈ ਅਤਿ, ਕਾਹੇ ਕਉ ਕੌਸਲ ਕੁੱਖ ਜਯੋ ਜੂ?

ਕਾਲ ਹੂ ਕਾਨ ਕਹੈ ਜਿਹਿ ਕੋ ਕਿਹਿ ਕਾਰਨੁ ਕਾਲ ਤੇ ਦੀਨ ਭਯੋ ਜੂ?

ਸੰਤ ਸਰੂਪ ਬਿਬੈਰ ਕਹਾਇ, ਸੁ ਕਿਯੋਂ ਪਥ ਕੋ ਰਥ ਹਾਕ ਧਯੋ ਜੂ?

ਤਾਹੀ ਕੋ ਮਾਨਿ ਪ੍ਰਭੂ ਕਰਿਕੈ ਜਿਹਿ ਕੋ ਕੋਊ ਭੇਦ ਨ ਲੇ, ਨ ਲਯੋ ਜੂ ॥੧੩॥

20. Savaiye

Jo kaho Ram ajon ajai at, kahay kau Kausal kukh jayo joo?

Kaal hoo Kaan kahay jih ko, kih kaaran kaal tay deen bhayo joo ?

Sant saroop bibair kahai, su kiyo path ko rath haak dhayo joo ?

Tahi ko maan Prabhu karkay, jih ko kou bhed na lai, na lalyo joo. 13 (713)

20. Savaiye (Tatees Savaiye, 13)

If you maintain that the all-Pervading God is unborn and invincible, how could He as Rama be born of the womb of Kaushalya ?[1]

And how is it that Krishna whom you call the Immortal God was helpless at the hands of Death ?[2]

And how is it that the All Holy and Revengeless Lord as Krishna drove the chariot of Arjana to battle ?[3]

Therefore, regard Him only as God whose mysteries none has been or will be able to unravel.13 (713)

---

1. **Rama** was born and therefore he cannot be identified with God who is unborn and not subject to death.
2. **Krishna** died and therefore he cannot be identified with God who is not subject to death.
3. **Krishna** helped Arjan to fight against his enemies. God is free from enmity and therefore Krishna cannot be called God.

21. ਸਵੱਯੇ ॥

ਕਿਯੋ ਕਹੁ ਕ੍ਰਿਸ਼ਨ ਕ੍ਰਿਪਾਨਿਧਿ ਹੈ? ਕਿਹ ਕਾਜਤੇ ਬਧਕ ਬਾਣ ਲਗਾਯੋ?
ਅਉਰ ਕੁਲੀਨ ਉਧਾਰਤ ਜੋ, ਕਿਹ ਤੇ ਅਪਨੋ ਕੁਲ ਨਾਸ਼ੁ ਕਰਾਯੋ?
ਆਦਿ ਅਜੋਨ ਕਹਾਇ, ਕਹੋ, ਕਿਮ ਦੇਵਕ ਕੇ ਜਠਰੰਤਰ ਆਯੋ?
ਤਾਤ ਨ ਮਾਤ ਕਹੋ ਜਿਹ ਕੋ, ਤਿਹ ਕਿਯੋ ਬਸੁਦੇਵਹ ਬਾਪ ਕਹਾਯੋ? ॥੧੪॥

21. Savaiye

Kiyo kah Krishan kirpanidh hai ? kih kaaj tay badhak baan lagaayo ?

Aur kuleen udhaarat jo, kih tay apno kul naas karaayo ?

Aad, ajon kahai kaho, kim Devak kay jathhrantar aayo ?

Taat na maat kaho jih ko, tih kiyo Basudevah baap kahaayo ? 14 (714)

21. Savaiye (Tatees Savaiye, 14)

How do you say that Krishna was God, the All Merciful ?

How is it that he was shot with an arrow of the hunter ?[1]

When he is said to be the saviour of other families, how come that he could not save his own family from destruction ?

God is called Primal and Unborn, then how can His coming into the womb of Devaki be explained.

God is without father and mother, but Krishna had a father named Vasudev.[2]

(714)

---

1. According to tradition, a hunter mistook the lotus foot of Krishna for the eye of a deer in the jungle and shot him.
2. God is not subject to birth; hence Krishna who was born to Devaki, and whose father was Vasudev cannot be called God.

22. ਵਾਰ ਦੁਰਗਾ । ਪਉੜੀ ।।

ਖੰਡਾ ਪ੍ਰਿਥਮਿ ਮਨਾਇਕੈ ਜਿਨ ਸਭ ਸੈਸਾਰ ਉਪਾਇਆ ।
ਬ੍ਰਹਮਾ ਬਿਸ਼ਨ ਮਹੇਸ਼ ਸਾਜਿ ਕੁਦਰਤਿ ਦਾ ਖੇਲ ਬਣਾਇਆ ।
ਚੌਦਾਂ ਤਬਕੈ ਬਣਾਇ ਕੈ, ਕੁਦਰਤਿ ਦਾ ਖੇਲ ਦਿਖਾਇਆ ।
ਸਿੰਧੁ ਪਰਬਤ ਮੇਦਨੀ ਬਿਨ ਥੰਮਾਂ ਗਗਨ ਰਹਾਇਆ ।
ਸਿਰਜੇ ਦਾਨੋ ਦੇਵਤੇ, ਤਿਨ ਅੰਦਰਿ ਬਾਦੁ ਰਚਾਇਆ ।
ਤੈ ਹੀ ਦੁਰਗਾ ਸਾਜਕੈ, ਦੈਂਤਾਂ ਦਾ ਨਾਸ ਕਰਾਇਆ ।
ਤੈਥੋਂ ਹੀ ਬਲੁ ਰਾਮ ਲੈ, ਨਾਲ ਬਾਣਾਂ ਰਾਵਣੁ ਘਾਇਆ ।
ਤੈਥੋਂ ਹੀ ਬਲੁ ਕ੍ਰਿਸਨ ਲੈ, ਕੰਸ ਕੇਸੀ ਪਕੜਿ ਗਿਰਾਇਆ ।
ਬਡੇ ਬਡੇ ਮੁਨਿ ਦੇਵਤੇ, ਕਈ ਜੁੱਗ ਤਿਨੀ ਤਨ ਤਾਇਆ ।
ਕਿਨੈ ਤੇਰਾ ਅੰਤੁ ਨ ਪਾਇਆ ।।੨।।

22. Vaar Durga : Pauri

Khandaa prithum manaai kay, jin sabh saisaar upaaiya,
Brahmaa Bishan Mahesh saaj, Kudrat daa khel banaaiya,
Chaudah tabkay banaai kay, Kudrat da khel dikhaaiya,
Sindh parbat medni, bin thamaa gagan rahaaiya.
Sirjay daano devtay, tin andar baad rachaaiya.
Tai hi Durga saj kay, Daitaa daa naas karaaiya.
Taithho hi bal Raam lai, naal baanaa Raavan ghaaiya
Taitho, hi bal Krishan lai, Kans kesi pakar giraaiya.
Baday baday munn devtay, kaee jug tinee tan taaiya.
Kinai teraa ant na paaiya. 2. (154)

22. Vaar Durga Pauri

First, God created the double-edged Dagger[1]
and, then, the universe.
He it is who created Brahma, Vishnu and Shiva,
and evolved the play of nature.
He created the fourteen regions[2]
and displayed the variety of nature
And created also the earth, mountains and oceans,
and vaulted the sky over us without a support.
And created also He the gods and demons,
and ploughed into their beings the germs of strife.
He it was who created Durga, the goddess of power,
and caused the demons to be destroyed.
It is from You, O God, that Rama received his prowess
to kill with his arrows the ten-headed Ravana,
'Tis you who bestowed Krishna with the power to
catch Kansa by the hair and destroy him.
Gods and ascetics and seers there were many upon many who
macerated themselves for Your sake, age after age.
But, Your limits, O God, no one has found ! 2

---

1. The "Source of Power". "Bhagauti" both in the creative and destructive aspects.
2. According to traditional belief there are seven upper regions and seven lower regions.

23. ਤੇਤੀਸ ਸਵੱਯੇ ॥

ਸੱਤਿ ਸਦੈਵ ਸਰੂਪ ਸਤੱਬ੍ਰਿਤ, ਆਦਿ ਅਨਾਦਿ ਅਗਾਧ ਅਜੈ ਹੈ ।
ਦਾਨ ਦਯਾ ਦਮ ਸੰਜਮ ਨੇਮ, ਜਤਬ੍ਰੱਤ ਸੀਲ ਸੁ ਥੱਤ ਅਬੈ ਹੈ ।
ਆਦਿ ਅਨੀਲ ਅਨਾਦ ਅਨਾਹਦ, ਆਪਿ ਅਦ੍ਰੈਖ ਅਭੇਖ ਅਭੈ ਹੈ ॥
ਰੂਪ ਅਰੂਪ ਅਰੇਖ ਜਰਾਰਦਨ, ਦੀਨ ਦਯਾਲ ਕ੍ਰਿਪਾਲ ਭਏ ਹੈ ॥੨॥

23. Tetees Savaiye

Sat sadev Saroop satbrat, aad anaad agaadh ajai hai.

Daan dayaa dam sanyam nem, jatbrat seel su thrat abai hai.

Aad aneel anaad anaahad, aap adwekh abhekh abhai hai.

Roop aroop arekh jaraardan, deen dayaal kripaal bhae hai. 2 (714)

23. Tatees Savaiye

God's existence is eternal, His laws endure; He is from the beginning, but Himself without a beginning. He is unfathomable and unconquerable.

His bounty, mercy, self-control, self-restraint, laws, vow of celibacy, and excellent vow of goodness never fail.

He is primeval, of no colour, without beginning, without end, self-begotten, boundless, without jealousy and without fear.

His form is formlessness. He hath no lines, is unaffected by old age, is merciful to the lowly and is all-kindness. 2

24. ਰਾਮਕਲੀ ਪਾਤਸ਼ਾਹੀ ੧੦

ਪ੍ਰਾਨੀ ਪਰਮ ਪੁਰਖ ਪਗ ਲਾਗੋ।।
ਸੋਵਤ ਕਹਾ ਮੋਹ ਨਿੰਦ੍ਰਾ ਮੈ ਕਬਹੂੰ ਸੁਚਿਤ ਹੈ ਜਾਗੋ।।੧।ਰਹਾਉ।।
ਔਰਨ ਕਹ ਉਪਦੇਸਤ ਹੈ ਪਸੁ ਤੋਹਿ ਪ੍ਰਬੋਧ ਨ ਲਾਗੋ।।
ਸਿੰਚਤ ਕਹਾ ਪਰੇ ਬਿਖਿਯਨ ਕਹ ਕਬਹੂ ਬਿਖੈ ਰਸ ਤਜਾਗੋ।।੧।।
ਕੇਵਲ ਕਰਮ ਭਰਮ ਸੇ ਚੀਨਹੁ ਧਰਮ ਕਰਮ ਅਨੁਰਾਗੋ।।
ਸੰਗ੍ਰਹਿ ਕਰੋ ਸਦਾ ਸਿਮਰਨ ਕੋ ਪਰਮ ਪਾਪ ਤਜਿ ਭਾਗੋ।।੨।।
ਜਾਤੇ ਦੂਖ ਪਾਪ ਨਹਿ ਭੇਟੈ ਕਾਲ ਜਾਲ ਤੇ ਤਾਗੋ।।
ਜੋ ਸੁਖ ਚਾਹੋ ਸਦਾ ਸਭਨ ਕੌ ਤੌ ਹਰਿ ਕੇ ਰਸ ਪਾਗੋ।।੩।।੩।।

24. Ramkali Patshahi Dasvee

Praani param purakh pag laago.

Sovat kahaa moh nindraa mai kabahoo suchit havai jaago. ? 1. Rahau.

Auaran kah updesat hai pus toh prabodh na laago.

Sinchat kahaa paray bikhian kah kabah bikhai ras tiyaago. 1.

Kewal karam bharam say cheenah dharam karam anuraago.

Sangrah karo sadaa simran ko param paap taj bhaago. 2.

Jatay dookh paap nah bhetai kaal jaal tay taago.

Jo sukh chaaho sadaa sabhan kau tau Har kay ras paago. 3, 3. (710)

SECTION II
HOLY NAME

24. Ramkali (Shabad Hazare)

O man, dedicate yourself to God's feet (commands).

Why are you asleep, intoxicated by worldly attachment?

Be awake and alert some times. 1. Pause.

O animal-like man, why do you have to preach to others, when you yourself do not follow the teaching?

Why are you amassing sins?[1] For some time (at least) forsake their poisonous relish .1.

Regard rituals as myths and superstitions and devote yourself to truly holy deeds.

Amass the (wealth of the) True Name; shun and flee from deadly sins.2.

In this manner, misery and sins will not affect you and you will be saved from the noose of Death.

If you desire eternal happiness for all, devote yourself to God's Name-Nectar. 3. (710)

---

1. In the pursuit of wealth and ambition, man commits lots of sins and crimes.

25. ਰਾਗੁ ਦੇਵ ਗੰਧਾਰੀ

ਬਿਨ ਹਰਿ ਨਾਮ ਨ ਬਾਚਨ ਪੈਹੈ ॥
ਚੌਦਹ ਲੋਕ ਜਾਹਿ ਬਸਿ ਕੀਨੇ ਤਾ ਤੇ ਕਹਾਂ ਪਲੈ ਹੈ ॥੧॥ ਰਹਾਉ ॥
ਰਾਮ ਰਹੀਮ ਉਬਾਰ ਨ ਸਕਿ ਹੈ ਜਾਕਰ ਨਾਮ ਰਟੈ ਹੈ ॥
ਬ੍ਰਹਮਾ ਬਿਸਨੁ ਰੁਦ੍ਰ ਸੂਰਜ ਸਸਿ ਤੇ ਬਸਿ ਕਾਲ ਸਭੈ ਹੈ ॥੧॥
ਬੇਦ ਪੁਰਾਨ ਕੁਰਾਨ ਸਭੈ ਮਤ ਜਾਕਹ ਨੇਤਿ ਕਹੈ ਹੈ ।
ਇੰਦ੍ਰ ਫਨਿੰਦ੍ਰ ਮੁਨਿੰਦ੍ਰ ਕਲਪ ਬਹੁ ਧਿਆਵਤ ਧਿਆਨ ਨ ਐਹੈ ॥੨॥
ਜਾਕਰ ਰੂਪ ਰੰਗ ਨਹਿ ਜਨਿਯਤ ਸੋ ਕਿਮ ਸਜਾਮ ਕਹੈ ਹੈ ॥
ਛੁਟਹੋ ਕਾਲ ਜਾਲ ਤੇ ਤਬਹੀ ਤਾਹਿ ਚਰਨ ਲਪਟੈ ਹੈ ॥੩॥੨॥

25. Raag Devagandhari

Bin Har Naam na baachan pai hai.
Chaudah lok jaah bas keenay ta tay kahaa palai hai. 1. Rahau.
Ram Rahim Ubaar na sak hai jaakar naam ratai hai.
Brahma Bisan Rudr Sooraj Sas tay bas kaal sabhai hai. 1.
Bed Puran Quran sabhai mat jaakah net kahai hai.
Indra, phunindra, munindra kalap bauh dhiavat dhian na aihai. 2.
Jaakar roop rang nah janyat so kim siyaam kahai hai.
Chhutiho kaal jaal tay tabahi taah charan laptai hai. 3,2. (711)

25. Raag Devagandhari (Shabad Hazare)

Without God's Name none can be liberated.

How can you escape from God's sway for He rules over the fourteen worlds.[1] Pause.

Ram and Rahim whose names you recite again and again—can not save you.

Brahma, Vishnu, Shiva[2], the Sun and the Moon are under the control of Death.

Vedas, Puranas, the Quran and all the religious denominations call God, Infinite.

Indra,[3] Shesh Nag,[4] the Leader of Munis meditated for long, but could not attain to Him.

How can God who has no colour or form be called blue-eyed[5] (Shyam)?

If you devotedly attach yourself to the feet of God, You will be saved from the noose of Death.[6]

(711)

---

1. According to tradition, there are fourteen worlds : seven in the upper region and seven in the nether region.
2. **Shiva** : The third of the Hindu Trinity, known as the Destroyer.
3. **Indra** : The King of Heaven, also god of rain.
4. **Shesh Nag** : The mythological multi-hooded cobra said to be the king of the nether world.
5. This has a reference to Lord Krishna who is known as Shyam.
6. Salvation implies the end of the cycle of death and birth and union with the Lord.

26. ਸਵੱਯੇ ॥

ਕਾਹੇ ਕੋ ਪੂਜਤ ਪਾਹਨ ਕਉ? ਕਛੁ ਪਾਹਨ ਕੈ ਪਰਮੇਸਰ ਨਾਹੀ ॥
ਤਾਹੀ ਕੋ ਪੂਜ ਪ੍ਰਭੂ ਕਰਕੈ ਜਿਹ ਪੂਜਤ ਹੀ ਅਘ ਓਘ ਮਿਟਾਹੀ ॥
ਆਧਿ ਬਿਆਧਿ ਕੇ ਬੰਧਨ ਜੇਤਕ ਨਾਮ ਕੇ ਲੇਤ ਸਭੈ ਛੁਟ ਜਾਹੀ ॥
ਤਾਹੀਂ ਕੋ ਧਿਆਨ ਪ੍ਰਮਾਨ ਸਦਾ ਇਨ ਫੋਕਟ ਧਰਮ ਕਰੇ ਫਲੁ ਨਾਹੀ ॥੨੦॥

26. Savaiye

Kahay ko poojat paahan kau ? Kachh paahan kai Parmesar naahee.
Tahi ko pooj Prabhu karkay jih poojat hi agh ogh mitahee.
Aadh biaabh kay bandhan jetak Naam kay lait sabhai chhut jaahee.
Taahee ko dhian pramaan sadaa in fokat dharam karay fal nahee. 20

(714)

26. Tatees Savaiye

Why do you worship stones ? How can God be contained in a stone ?

Worship Him, the only Lord, by worshipping whom all pains and sins vanish,

By remembering whose Name, all physical and mental ills shall vanish.

Meditation on God alone is acceptable, and other vain deeds bring no fruit.   20.   (714)

27. ਸਵੱਯੇ ॥

ਬੇਦ ਕਤੇਬ ਨ ਬੇਦ ਲਹਿਯੋ ਤਿਹਿ, ਸਿੱਧ ਸਮਾਧਿ ਸਬੈ ਕਰਿ ਹਾਰੇ ॥
ਸਿਮ੍ਰਿਤਿ ਸਾਸਤ੍ਰ ਬੇਦ ਸਬੈ, ਬਹੁ ਭਾਂਤਿ ਪੁਰਾਨ ਬੀਚਾਰ ਬੀਚਾਰੇ ॥
ਆਦਿ ਅਨਾਦਿ ਅਗਾਧਿ ਕਥਾ, ਧ੍ਰੂਅ ਸੋ ਪ੍ਰਹਲਾਦਿ ਅਜਾਮਲ ਤਾਰੇ ॥
ਨਾਮ ਉਚਾਰ ਤਰੀ ਗਨਿਕਾ, ਸੋਈ ਨਾਮੁ ਅਧਾਰ ਬੀਚਾਰ ਹਮਾਰੇ ॥੧੦॥

27. Sayaiye

Bed kateb na bhed lahiyo tih, sidh samaadh sabai kar haaray.
Simrit sastar bed sabai, bah bhant puran beechar beecharay.
Aad anaad agaadh kathaa, Dhru say Prahlad Ajaamal taaray.
Naam uchaar taree Ganika, soi Naam adhaar beechar hamaaray. 10.

(713)

27. Savaiye (Tatees Savaiye 10)

The Vedas and the Katebas have failed to explain God's mystery. Siddhas have failed to attain to Him through contemplation.

The Simiritis, the Shastras, the Vedas and the Puranas have conjectured the aspects of God in different ways.

He, the Primal Being, who is without origin and beyond description, saved Dhru[1], Ajamal[2] and Prahlad.[3]

The Holy Name which saved Ganika[4] the prostitute is the basis of all my support. 10 (713)

---

1. **Dhru** : An ancient Indian sage who was the son of King Uttanpada.
2. **Ajamal** : A sinful man who, according to tradition has a son called Narayan. On his death-bed he called his son Narayan (which means God) and he was liberated.
3. **Prahlad** : An Indian saint who was harassed by his father Harnakash. Vishnu appeared from a pillar in the form of Man-lion and tore Harnakash to pieces.
4. **Ganika** : A prostitute whom a saint gave a parrot which could utter "Ram". She remembered the parrot's word "Ram" which stands for God, at the time of her death and was thus saved.

28. ਤ੍ਵ ਪ੍ਰਸਾਦਿ ॥ ਸਵੱਯੇ ॥

ਸ੍ਰਾਵਗ ਸੁੱਧ ਸਮੂਹ ਸਿਧਾਨ ਕੇ ਦੇਖਿ ਫਿਰਿਓ ਘਰ ਜੋਗ ਜਤੀ ਕੇ ॥

ਸੂਰ ਸੁਰਾਰਦਨ ਸੁੱਧ ਸੁਧਾਦਿਕ ਸੰਤ ਸਮੂਹ ਅਨੇਕ ਮਤੀ ਕੇ ॥

ਸਾਰੇ ਹੀ ਦੇਸ ਕੋ ਦੇਖਿ ਰਹਿਓ ਮਤ ਕੋਉ ਨ ਦੇਖੀਅਤ ਪ੍ਰਾਨ ਪਤੀ ਕੇ ॥

ਸ੍ਰੀ ਭਗਵਾਨ ਕੀ ਭਾਇ ਕ੍ਰਿਪਾ ਹੂੰ ਤੇ ਏਕ ਰਤੀ ਬਿਨ ਏਕ ਰਤੀ ਕੇ ॥੧॥੨੧॥

28. Tav Prasad Savaiye

Sraavag sudh samooh sidhaan kay, dekh firio ghar jog jatee kay.

Soor suraardan sudh sudhaadik, sant samooh anek matee kay.

Saaray hi des ko dekh rahio mat, kou na dekhiat Praan pati kay.

Sri Bhagwaan kee bhai kripaa hu tay, ek ratee bin ek ratee kay. 1. 21.

(13)

SECTION III
FALSE RELIGION

28. Tav Prasaad Savaiye

I have gone into the houses of saravags[1] suddhs[2], siddhas[3], yogis[4] and Jatis.[5]

I have also come across groups of warrior-demons, nectar-loving gods, and holy men of different sects.

I have examined the religions of various countries, but none of them preaches the true devotion to God, the Lord of Life.

All these religions are good for nothing, if they cannot win the love and grace of God. 1.21 (13)

---

1. **Saravags** are sect of Jains who deliberately remain dirty.
2. **Suddhs** are a religious sect who keep very clean.
3. **Siddhas** are a sect of Yogis who possess occult powers.
4. **Yogis** are ascetics who practise austerities, physical and meditational exercises.
5. **Jatis** are a religious sect who remain celibate and keep away from women.

29. ਤ੍ਵ ਪ੍ਰਸਾਦਿ ।। ਸਵੱਯੇ ।।

ਤੀਰਥ ਨ੍ਹਾਨ ਦਯਾ ਦਮ ਦਾਨ ਸੁ ਸੰਜਮ ਨੇਮ ਅਨੇਕ ਬਿਸੇਖੈ ।।
ਬੇਦ ਪੁਰਾਨ ਕਤੇਬ ਕੁਰਾਨ ਜਿਮੀਨ ਜਮਾਨ ਸਬਾਨ ਕੇ ਪੇਖੈ ।।
ਪੌਨ ਅਹਾਰ ਜਤੀ ਜਤ ਧਾਰ ਸਬੈ ਸੁ ਬਿਚਾਰ ਹਜਾਰਕ ਦੇਖੈ ।।
ਸ੍ਰੀ ਭਗਵਾਨ ਭਜੇ ਬਿਨ ਭੂਪਤਿ ਏਕ ਰਤੀ ਬਿਨ ਏਕ ਨ ਲੇਖੈ ।।੪।।੨੪।।

29. Tav Prassad Savaiye

Teerath naan daya dam daan, su sanjam nem anek bisaykhai.
Bed Puran Kateb Quran jameen jamaan sabaan kay pekhai.
Paun ahaar jatee jat dhaar, sabai su bichaar hajaarak dekhai.
Sri Bhagwaan bhajay bin bhupat ek rati bin ek na laykhai. 4, 24   (14)

29. Tav Prasaad Savaiye

If the individual were to bathe at different pilgrim-spots and do acts of compassion and were to discipline his passions, and perfrom acts of charity and practise self-control and participate in many rituals.

If he were to study the Vedas, the Puranas, the Quran and other religious scriptures of all countries and ages,

If he were to live only on air[1] and were to practise continence and perform thousands of ceremonies,

All these practices are profitless, without meditation on and love of the Creator. (14)

---

1. Living on air implies fasting. Fasting as such is not approved by the Sikh Gurus. It confers no spiritual benefit.

30. ਤੂ ਪ੍ਰਸਾਦਿ ॥ ਸਵੱਯੇ ॥

ਕਹਾ ਭਯੋ ਜੋ ਦੋਊ ਲੋਚਨ ਮੂੰਦ ਕੈ ਬੈਠਿ ਰਹਿਓ ਬਕ ਧਿਆਨ ਲਗਾਇਓ ॥
ਨ੍ਹਾਤ ਫਿਰਿਓ ਲੀਏ ਸਾਤ ਸਮੁੰਦ੍ਰਨ ਲੋਕ ਗਇਓ ਪਰਲੋਕ ਗਵਾਇਓ ॥
ਬਾਸ ਕੀਓ ਬਿਖਿਆਨ ਸੋ ਬੈਠਕੈ ਐਸੇ ਹੀ ਐਸੇ ਸੁ ਬੈਸ ਬਿਤਾਇਓ ॥
ਸਾਚੁ ਕਹੋਂ ਸੁਨ ਲੇਹੁ ਸਭੈ ਜਿਨ ਪ੍ਰੇਮ ਕੀਓ ਤਿਨਹੀ ਪ੍ਰਭੁ ਪਾਇਓ ॥੯॥੨੯॥

30. Tav Prasaad Savaiye

Kahaa bhaiyo jo dou lochan moond kay baith rahiyo bak dhian lagaaiyo.
Naat phirio liay saat samundran lok gaiyo parlok gavaaiyo.
Bass kio bikhiaan so baithkai aisay hi aisay so bais bitaaiyo.
Saach kahou sun laih sabhai jin prem kio tin hi Prabh paaiyo.   (14)

30. Tav Prasaad Savaiye

Of what use is sitting with closed eyes like a crane,[1] pretending to meditate ?

Those who go to pilgrimage and take baths in the seven seas[2] lose everything in this world and the next.

They misuse their time in doing evil things and thus waste away their lives.

I speak the Truth and let all listen to it : Those who love God alone will merge in Him. (14)

---

1. A crane generally keeps his eyes half-closed for catching fish. Similarly hypocritical preachers pretend to meditate with eyes half-closed and as soon as they find a rich disciple, they prey upon him.
2. The seven seas refer to numerous holy tanks and rivers.
    (Hyperbole is a figure of speech used generally in poetry.)

31. ਤੂ ਪ੍ਰਸਾਦਿ ॥ ਸਵੱਯੇ ॥

ਤੀਰਥ ਕੋਟ ਕੀਏ ਇਸਨਾਨ ਦੀਏ ਬਹੁ ਦਾਨ ਮਹਾ ਬ੍ਰਤ ਧਾਰੇ ॥
ਦੇਸ ਫਿਰਿਓ ਕਰਿ ਭੇਸ ਤਪੋ ਧਨ ਕੇਸ ਧਰੇ ਨ ਮਿਲੇ ਹਰਿ ਪਿਆਰੇ ॥
ਆਸਨ ਕੋਟ ਕਰੇ ਅਸਟਾਂਗ ਧਰੇ ਬਹੁ ਨਜਾਸ ਕਰੇ ਮੁਖ ਕਾਰੇ ॥
ਦੀਨ ਦਇਆਲ ਅਕਾਲ ਭਜੇ ਬਿਨ ਅੰਤ ਕੋ ਅੰਤ ਕੇ ਧਾਮ ਸਿਧਾਰੇ ॥੧੦॥

31. Tav Prasaad Savaiye

Teerath kot kiay isnaan deeay bauh daan mahaa brat dhaaray.

Des firio kar bhes tapo dhan kes dharay na milay Har piyaaray.

Aasan kot karay astang dharay bau niyas karay mukh kaaray.

Deen dayal Akaal bhajay bin ant ko ant kay dhaam sidhaaray. 10 (35)

31. Tav Prasaad Savaiye

Those who go to pilgrimage and take millions of baths, donate lots of things in charity and keep fasts,

Those who wearing penitential garbs and keeping long hair have wandered in different countries and not found God,

Those who practise millions of postures according to Ashtang Yoga[1] and make offerings of limbs and blacken their faces,

Without remembering the Name of the Compassionate and Immortal God, all of them will have to proceed to the place of the god of Death. (35)

---

1. Patanjali's system of Yoga is called Ashtang (eightfold) Yoga. It is based on eight principles as under:
   - (i) **Yama** : Practice of non-violence, truthfulness, non-covetousness, chastity and not receiving anything from another.
   - (ii) **Niyama** : Austerity, contentment, purity and worship of God.
   - (iii) **Asana** : Postures and physical exercise to keep the body healthy.
   - (iv) **Pranayama** : Control and purification of breathing.
   - (v) **Pratyahara** : Control of sense-organs by one's will.
   - (vi) **Dharna** : Holding the mind on some point or idea.
   - (vii) **Dhyana** : Meditation on the deity or God.
   - (viii) **Samadhi** : Condition of trance where one gets in tune with God.

32. ਤੇਤੀਸ ਸਵੱਯੇ ॥

ਕਾਹੂ ਲੈ ਠੋਕ ਬਧੇ ਉਰ ਠਾਕੁਰ, ਕਾਹੂ ਮਹੇਸ ਕੋ ਏਸ ਬਖਾਨਿਯੋ ।

ਕਾਹੂ ਕਹਿਯੋ ਹਰਿ ਮੰਦਰ ਮੈ ਹਰਿ, ਕਾਹੂ ਮਸੀਤ ਕੇ ਬੀਚ ਪ੍ਰਮਾਨਿਯੋ ।

ਕਾਹੂ ਨੇ ਰਾਮ ਕਹਿਯੋ, ਕ੍ਰਿਸਨਾ ਕਾਹੂੰ, ਕਾਹੂ ਮਨੈ ਅਵਤਾਰਨ ਮਾਨਿਯੋ ।

ਫੋਕਟ ਧਰਮ ਬਿਸਾਰ ਸਬੈ ਕਰਤਾਰ ਹੀ ਕਉ ਕਰਤਾ ਜੀਅ ਜਾਨਿਯੋ ॥੧੨॥

32. Tatees Savaiye

Kaahoo lai thhok badhai ur thakur, Kahoo mahes ko es bakhaanio.

Kaahoo kahiyo har mandar mai Har,

Kaahoo maseet kay beech pramaanio.

Kahoo ne Raam Kahio, Krishna kaahoo, Kahoo manai avtaaran maanio.

Fokat Dharam bisaar sabai,

Kartaar hee kau kartaa jeea jaanio. 12

32. Tatees Savaiye

Some firmly believe in the images of Vishnu, others call Shiva their Lord.

Some consider God's abode to be a temple, others fix His residence in a mosque.

Some call him Rama, some Krishna, other identify Him in their minds with other incarnations.

Abandoning all these barren ways, I believe the Creator only to be the Lord of all beings. 12 (714)

33. ਤੇਤੀਸ ਸੱਵਯੇ ॥

ਜੌਂ ਜੁਗ ਤੈ ਕਰਹੈ ਤਪਸਾ, ਕੁਛ ਤੋਹਿ ਪ੍ਰਸੰਨ ਨ ਪਾਹਨ ਕੈ ਹੈ ।
ਹਾਥ ਉਠਾਇ ਭਲੀ ਬਿਧਿ ਸੋ, ਜੜ! ਤੋਹਿ ਕਛੂ ਬਰਦਾਨ ਨ ਦੇ ਹੈ ।
ਕੌਨ ਭਰੋਸ ਭਯਾ ਇਹ ਕੋ? ਕਹੁ, ਬੀਰ ਪਰੀ ਨਹਿ ਆਨਿ ਬਚੈ ਹੈ ।
ਜਾਨ ਰੇ ਜਾਨ! ਅਜਾਨ ਹਠੀ! ਇਹ ਫੋਕਟ ਧਰਮ ਸੁ ਭਰਮ ਗਵੈ ਹੈ ॥੨੨॥

33. Tatees Savaiye

Jo jug tai karahai tapasaa, Kuchh toh prasan na paahan kai hai.
Haath uthhaai bhalee bidh so jar ! Toh kachhoo bardaan na day hai.
Kon bharos bhayaa ih ko ? kah, Bhir paree nah aan bachai hai.
Jaan ray jaan ! ajaan hathhee ! Eh fokat dharam su bharam gavai hai.

22. (715)

33. Tatees Sayaiye

For eons you may worship a stone, but

it will not gladden your heart.

The image will not confer any boon upon you, with its arms uplifted in a gracious manner, O dullard !

Tell me, how did you come to repose any trust in it ? It never helped you in trouble. 22.

O stubborn wretch, beware; this fruitless ritual will hasten your doom.

22.

34. ਤੇਤੀਸ ਸਵੱਯੇ ॥

ਜਾਲ ਬਧੇ ਸਬ ਹੀ ਮ੍ਰਿਤਕੇ ਕੋਊ ਰਾਮ ਰਸੂਲ ਨ ਬਾਚਨ ਪਾਏ ॥

ਦਾਨਵ ਦੇਵ ਫਨਿੰਦ੍ਰ ਧਰਾਧਰ ਭੂਤ ਭਵਿੱਖ ਉਪਾਇ ਮਿਟਾਏ ॥

ਅੰਤ ਮਰੈ ਪਛਤਾਇ ਪ੍ਰਿਥੀ ਪਰਿ ਜੇ ਜਗ ਮੈ ਅਵਤਾਰ ਕਹਾਏ ॥

ਰੇ ਮਨ ਲੈਲ!

ਇਕੇਲ ਹੀ ਕਾਲ ਕੇ ਲਾਗਤ ਕਾਹਿ ਨ ਪਾਇਨ ਧਾਏ? ॥੨੩॥

34. Tatees Savaiye

Jaal badhay sab hi mrit kay kou Ram Rasul na baachan paay.

Danav dev phanindra dharadhar bhoot bhavikh upai mitaay.

Ant maray pachhtai prithi par jay jag mai avtaar kahaay.

Ray man lail ?

Ikel hi kaal kay lagat kah na paen dhaay ?   23   (715)

34. Savaiye (Tatees Savaiye)

All were entangled in the net-work of death. No Rama or any prophet could escape it.

The gods, demons, serpents and mountains were created and destroyed in the past and will be created and destroyed in the future too.

Those who declared themselves as God's incarnations[1] died lamenting in the end on this earth.

O fickle mind ! Why do you then not bow at the feet of the Destroyer (God) alone ? (715)

---

1. **Guru Gobind Singh** did not believe in incarnations of God, because God is not subject to birth and death.

35. ਤੇਤੀਸ ਸਵੱਯੇ ॥

ਕਾਲ ਗਯੋ ਇਨ ਕਾਮਨ ਸਿਉ, ਜੜ!
ਕਾਲ ਕ੍ਰਿਪਾਲ ਹੀਐ ਨ ਚਿਤਾਰਿਯੋ।
ਲਾਜ ਸੋ ਛਾਡ, ਨਿਲਾਜ ਅਰੇ!
ਤਜਿ ਕਾਜ, ਅਕਾਜ ਕੋ ਕਾਜ ਸਵਾਰਿਯੋ।
ਬਾਜ ਬਨੈ ਗਜਰਾਜ ਬਡੇ,
ਖਰਕੋ ਚੜ੍ਹਬੋਚਿਤ ਬੀਚ ਬੀਚਾਰਿਯੋ।
ਸ੍ਰੀ ਭਗਵੰਤ ਭਜਿਯੋ ਨ, ਅਰੇ ਜੜੂ!
ਲਾਜ ਹੀ ਲਾਜ ਹੀ ਕਾਜ ਬਿਗਾਰਿਯੋ॥੨੫॥

35. Tatees Savaiye

Kaal gayo in kaaman siu jar,

Kaal kripaal heeai na chitaario.

Laaj so chhaad, nilaaj aray !

Taj kaaj, akaaj ko kaaj savaariyo.

Baaj banay gajraaj baday,

Kharke charhbochit beech bichaariyo.

Sri Bhagwant bhajio na aray jar !

Laaj hee laaj hee kaaj bigaario 25. (715)

35. Tatees Savaiye

You did waste time in these deeds, unthinking man! and did never remember the merciful Lord.

You did banish all feelings of shame O shameless one ! and leaving your proper work committed evil deeds, bringing no fruit to you.

You had beautiful horses and huge elephants, but you to ride an ass.

Know, foolish person ! know this barren path is of ignorance. You lost the chance and never meditated on the supreme Lord . 25.   (715)

36. ਸਵੱਯੇ ॥

ਬੇਦ ਕਤੇਬ ਪੜ੍ਹੇ ਬਹੁਤੇ ਦਿਨ ਭੇਦ ਕਛੁ ਤਿਨ ਕੋ ਨਹਿ ਪਾਇਯੋ ।
ਪੂਜਤ ਠੌਰ ਅਨੇਕ ਫਿਰਿਯੋ, ਪਰ ਏਕ ਕਬੈ ਹੀਯ ਮੈ ਨ ਬਸਾਯੋ ।
ਪਾਹਨ ਕੋ ਅਸਥਾਲਯ ਕੋ ਸਿਰਿ ਨਿਯਾਇ ਫਿਰਿਯੋ ਕਛੁ ਹਾਬਿ ਨ ਆਯੋ ।
ਰੇ ਮਨ ਮੂੜ੍ਹ! ਅਗੂੜ, ਪ੍ਰਭੁ ਤਜਿ, ਆਪਨ ਹੂੜ ਕਹਾ ਉਰਝਾਯੋ?॥੨੬॥

36. Sayaiye

Bed kateb parhay bahutay din bhed kachhoo tin ko nah paaiyo.
Poojat thaur anek firio par ek kabai hia mai na basaayo.
Paahan ko asthaliya ko sirr niyai firio kachh haath na aayo.
Ray man moorh ! agoorh Prabhu taj, aapan hoor kaha urjhaayo ? 26

(715)

36. Savaiye (Tatees Savaiye)

For several days, you have read the Vedas and Katebas[1] but still have not understood their inner meaning.

You worshipped one god after another and moved from place to place, but never thought of cherishing the one Lord in your heart.

You have bowed to stones and shrines, but gained nothing.

O foolish mind ! Why have you forsaken the mighty Lord and entangled yourself in vain pursuits ? (715)

---

1. **Katebas :** The reference is to the Semitic scriptures, four in number, namely **Jabur** of prophet Daud (David). **Tohra** of prophet (Moses), **Bible** of prophet Christ, and **Quran** of prophet Mohammed.

37. ਸਵੱਯੇ ॥

ਜੋ ਜੁਗੀਆਨ ਕੇ ਜਾਇ, ਕਹੈ, – "ਸਭਿ ਜੋਗਨ ਕੋ ਗ੍ਰਿਹ ਮਾਲ ਉਠੈ ਦੈ"॥

ਜੋ ਪਰੋ ਭਾਜਿ ਸੰਨਿਯਾਸਨ ਦੈ ਕਹੈਂ, – "ਦਤ ਕੈ ਨਾਮ ਪੈ ਧਾਮ ਲੁਟੈਦੈ"॥

ਜੋ ਕਰਿ ਕੋਉ ਮਸੰਦਨ ਸੋ, ਕਹੈਂ, – "ਸਰਬ ਦਰਬ ਲੈ ਮੋਹਿ ਅਬੈਦੈ"।

ਲੇਉ ਹੀ ਲੇਉ ਕਹੈ ਸਭ ਕੋ ਨਰ, ਕੋਉ ਨ ਬ੍ਰਹਮ ਬਤਾਇ ਹਮੈ ਦੈ॥੨੮॥

37. Savaiye

Jo jugiaan kay jaae kahai : " Sabh jogan ko grih maal uthhai dai."

Jo paro bhaaj sanyasan dai kahai : "Datt kai naam pai dhaam lutai dai".

Jo kar kou massandan so kahai : " Sarab darab lai moh abai dai."

Leh hi leh kahai sabh ko nar, kou na Brahm batai hamai dai. 28   (715)

37. Savaiye (Tatees Savaiye)

If one goes to the Yogis, they will ask him to surrender all his wealth to them.

If one runs to the Sanyasis, they will tell him to renounce all his property in the name of Datta.[1]

If one goes to the Massands[2] they will at once demand all his goods.

They all say : "Give us all", but there is none to give me the knowledge of God. (715)

---

1. **Dattatriya :** Datta for short -was the founder of a sect Sanyasis (ascetics).
2. **Massands :** This was an organisation of Sikh missionaries started by Guru Ramdas, but it was abolished by Guru Gobind Singh because the Massands had become corrupt and wicked.

38. ਸਵੱਯੇ ॥

ਆਂਖਨ ਭੀਤਰਿ ਤੇਲ ਕੌ ਡਾਰ ਸੁ ਲੋਗਨ ਨੀਰ ਬਹਾਇ ਦਿਖਾਵੈ ॥
ਜੋ ਧਨਵਾਨ ਲਖੈ ਨਿਜ ਸੇਵਕ ਤਾਹਿ ਪਰੋਸ ਪ੍ਰਸਾਦਿ ਜਿਮਾਵੈ ॥
ਜੋ ਧਨ ਹੀਨ ਲਖੇ ਹਿਤ ਦੇਤ ਨ, ਮਾਂਗਨ ਜਾਤ ਮੁਖੋ ਨ ਦਿਖਾਵੈ ॥
ਲੂਟਤ ਹੈ ਪਸੂ ਲੋਗਨ ਕੋ ਕਬਹੂੰ ਨ ਪ੍ਰਮੇਸ਼ਰ ਕੇ ਗੁਨ ਗਾਵੈ ॥੩੦॥

38. Savaiye

Aankhan bheetar tel ko daar, so logan neer bahai dikhaavai.
Jo dhanvaan lakhai nij sewak, tahi paros prasaad jimaavai.
Jo dhan heen lakhay hit det na, maangan jaat mukho na dikhaavai.
Lootat hai pasoo logan ko, kabahoo na Pramesar kay gun gaavai. 30

(715)

38. Savaiye (Tatees Savaiye)

People drop oil in their eyes[1] to show others that they are full of tears of sympathy for them.

When they see a rich disciple, they serve him with delicious food.

When a poor disciple goes to them, they pay no heed to his request and often hide their faces from him.

Such beasts[2] are looting the people. They never sing the praises of God. (716)

---
1. This was one of the devices employed by hypocritical preachers and sadhus to attract disciples.
2. Such fake religious teachers are called 'beasts' by Guru Gobind Singh.

39. ਸਵੱਯੇ ॥

ਫੋਕਟ ਕਰਮ ਦਿੜ੍ਹਾਤ ਕਹਾਂ ਇਨ ਲੋਗਨਕੌਂ? ਕੋਈ ਕਾਮ ਨ ਐਹੈ।
ਭਾਜਤ ਕਾ ਧਨ ਹੇਤ? ਅਰੇ! ਜਮ ਕਿੰਕਰ ਤੇ ਨਹਿ ਭਾਜਨ ਪੈਹੈ॥
ਪੁਤ੍ਰ ਕਲਿਤ੍ਰ ਨ ਮਿਤ੍ਰ ਸਬੈ ਉਹਾ ਸਿੱਖ ਸਖਾ ਕੋਉ ਸਾਖ ਨ ਦੈਹੈ॥
ਚੇਤ ਰੇ ਚੇਤ! ਅਚੇਤ ਮਹਾ ਪਸੂ! ਅੰਤ ਕੀ ਬਾਰ ਅਕੇਲੋ ਹੀ ਜੈ ਹੈ॥੩੨॥

39. Savaiye

Fokat karam dirhat kahaa in logan ko? koi kaam na ai hai.

Bhaajat kaa dhan het ? Aray ! jam kinkar tay nah bhaajan pai hai.

Putr kalitr na mitr sabai ooha sikh sakhaa kou saakh na dai hai.

Chet ray chet ! Achet mahaa pas ! Ant ki baar akelo hi jai hai. 32 (715)

39. Savaiye (Tatees Savaiye)

Why are you exhorting the people to perform actions which are useless?

Why are you running after wealth ? You will not be able to run away from the clutches of Death.

There in God's court, none will bear witness in your favour, not even your sons, wife, friends or disciples.

Think it over, O ignorant brute ! You shall have to go alone in the end.

(716)

40. ਤ੍ਰ ਪ੍ਰਸਾਦਿ ॥ ਸਵੱਯੇ ॥

ਮਾਤੇ ਮਤੰਗ ਜਰੇ ਜਰ ਸੰਗ ਅਨੂਪ ਉਤੰਗ ਸੁਰੰਗ ਸਵਾਰੇ ॥

ਕੋਟ ਤੁਰੰਗ ਕੁਰੰਗ ਸੇ ਕੂਦਤ ਪਉਨ ਕੇ ਗਉਨ ਕਉ ਜਾਤ ਨਿਵਾਰੇ ॥

ਭਾਰੀ ਭੁਜਾਨ ਕੇ ਭੂਪ ਭਲੀ ਬਿਧਿ ਨਿਆਵਤ ਸੀਸ ਨ ਜਾਤ ਬਿਚਾਰੇ ॥

ਏਤੇ ਭਏ ਤੋ ਕਹਾ ਭਏ ਭੂਪਤਿ ਅੰਤ ਕੌ ਨਾਂਗੇ ਹੀ ਪਾਇ ਪਧਾਰੇ ॥੨॥੨੨॥

40. Tav Prasaad Savaiye

Maatay matang jaray jar sung anoop utang surang savaray.

Kot turang kurang say koodat paun kay gaun kau jaat nivaaray.

Bhaaree bhujaan kay bhoop bhalee bidh niyaavat sees na jaat bichaaray.

Etay bhae to kahaa bhae bhoopat ant kou nangay hi pai padhaaray.

2.22 (13)

SECTION IV
TRANSITORY WORLD

40. Tav Prasaad Savaiye

Were emperors to possess tall and noble elephants, painted in beautiful colours and adorned with golden trappings.

Were emperors to possess millions of horses, galloping at speed faster than that of the wind and racing like the deer,

If other kings having powerful and long arms were to visit these emperors and bow their heads to them in submission,

It matters not if such powerful emperors existed, because at the end they left the world barefooted. (13)

41. ਤ੍ਵ ਪ੍ਰਸਾਦਿ।। ਸਵੱਯੇ।।

ਜੀਤ ਫਿਰੈ ਸਭ ਦੇਸ ਦਿਸਾਨ ਕੋ ਬਾਜਤ ਢੋਲ ਮ੍ਰਿਦੰਗ ਨਗਾਰੇ।।

ਗੂੰਜਤ ਗੂੜ ਗਜਾਨ ਕੇ ਸੁੰਦਰ ਹਿੰਸਤ ਹੀ ਹਯਰਾਜ ਹਜਾਰੇ।।

ਭੂਤ ਭਵਿੱਖ ਭਵਾਨ ਕੇ ਭੂਪਤਿ ਕਉਨੁ ਗਨੈ ਨਹੀ ਜਾਤ ਬਿਚਾਰੇ।।

ਸ੍ਰੀ ਪਤਿ ਸ੍ਰੀ ਭਗਵਾਨ ਭਜੇ ਬਿਨੁ ਅੰਤ ਕਉ ਅੰਤ ਕੇ ਧਾਮ ਸਿਧਾਰੇ।।੩।।੨੩।।

41. Tav Prasaad Savaiye

Jeet firai sabh des disaan ko baajat dhol mridang nagaaray.

Gunjat goor gajaan kay sundar hinsat hi hayaraaj hajaaray.

Bhoot bhavikh bhavaan kay bhoopat kaun ganay nahi jaat bichaaray.

Sri pat Sri Bhagwaan bhajay bin ant ko ant kay dhaam sidhaaray. 3.23

(13)

41. Tav Prasaad Savaiye

If mighty emperors were to go round and conquer all the countries, after beating different kinds of drums of war,

If a number of beautiful elephants were to trumpet boldly and if thousands of horses of high breed were to neigh (in their palaces).

Such emperors living in the past or in the present or likely to exist in the future cannot perhaps be correctly counted,

Yet without worshipping the Name of God, they have to leave (in utter helplessness) for their final home (of death) (31)

42. ਤ੍ਰ ਪ੍ਰਸਾਦਿ ॥ ਸਵੱਯੇ ॥

ਸੁੱਧ ਸਿਪਾਹ ਦੁਰੰਤ ਦੁਬਾਹ ਸੁ ਸਾਜਿ ਸਨਾਹ ਦੁਜਾਨ ਦਲੈਂਗੇ॥

ਭਾਰੀ ਗੁਮਾਨ ਭਰੇ ਮਨ ਮੈ ਕਰ ਪਰਬਤ ਪੰਖ ਹਲੈ ਨ ਹਲੈਂਗੇ॥

ਤੋਰ ਅਰੀਨ ਮਰੋਰ ਮਵਾਸਨ ਮਾਤੇ ਮਤੰਗਨ ਮਾਨ ਮਲੈਂਗੇ॥

ਸ੍ਰੀ ਪਤਿ ਸ੍ਰੀ ਭਗਵਾਨ ਕ੍ਰਿਪਾ ਬਿਨੁ ਤਿਆਗਿ ਜਹਾਨ ਨਿਦਾਨ ਚਲੈਂਗੇ॥੫॥੨੫॥

42. Tav Prasaad Savaiye

Sudh sipaah durant dubaah su saaj sanaah durjaan dalaingay.

Bhaaree gumaan bharay man mai kar parbat pankh halai na halaingay.

Tor areen maror mavaasan maatay matangan maan malaingay.

Sripat Sri Bhagwan kripa bin tiyag jahan nidaan chalaingay. 5. 25   (14)

42. Tav Prasaad Savaiye

If there were veteran, strong and invincible soldiers, equipped with coats of mail and capable of subduing the enemy.

If filled with conceit, they thought they would never quit the battle-field, even though hard mountains—if furnished with wings—could leave their places,[1]

If they were powerful to break into bits the revolting armies and twist their heads and even crush the pride of furious elephants.

Without the merciful glance of God, such brave soldiers would leave the world empty-handed. (14)

---
1. Even if mountains could move, the warriors would not quit the battle-field. They would keep their ground in spite of terrible enemy-pressure.

43. ਤੂ ਪ੍ਰਸਾਦਿ ॥ ਸਵੱਯੇ ॥

ਬੀਰ ਅਪਾਰ ਬਡੇ ਬਰਿਆਰ ਅਬਿਚਾਰਹਿ ਸਾਰ ਕੀ ਧਾਰ ਭਛੱਯਾ ॥
ਤੋਰਤ ਦੇਸ ਮਲਿੰਦ ਮਵਾਸਨ ਮਾਤੇ ਗਜਾਨ ਕੇ ਮਾਨ ਮਲੱਯਾ ॥
ਗਾੜ੍ਹੇ ਗੜ੍ਹਾਨ ਕੋ ਤੋੜਨਹਾਰ ਸੁਬਾਤਨ ਹੀ ਚਕ ਚਾਰ ਲਵੱਯਾ ॥
ਸਾਹਿਬ ਸ੍ਰੀ ਸਭ ਕੋ ਸਿਰ ਨਾਇਕ ਜਾਚਿਕ ਅਨੇਕ ਸੁ ਏਕ ਦਿਵੱਯਾ ॥੬॥੨੬॥

43. Tav Prasaad Savaiye

Beer apaar baday bariaar abcharah saar ki dhaar bhachhaiyaa.
Torat des malind mavaasan matay gajaan kay maan malaiyaa.
Garhay garhaan kay toranhaar su baatan hi chak chaar lavaiyaa.
Sahib Sri sabh ko sir naaik jaachik anek su ek divaiyaa. 6. 26   (14)

43. Tav Prasaad Savaiye

If there were numerous warriors, capable of touching the sharp edge of the sword ungrudgingly,

If they were to conquer several countries and defeat the rebels and break the pride of wild elephants,[1]

If they could destroy huge forts and capture the world simply by their boasts or threats,

Even so, God alone is the only Giver and Ruler of all. They stand like beggars at His court. (14)

---

1. Holding a wild elephant at bay was regarded as a great and glorious feat of a warrior.

44. ਤ੍ਰਪ੍ਰਸਾਦਿ।। ਸਵੱਯੇ।।

ਮਾਨਵ ਇੰਦ੍ਰ ਗਜਿੰਦ੍ਰ ਨਰਾਧਿਪ ਜੌਨ ਤ੍ਰਿਲੋਕ ਕੋ ਰਾਜੁ ਕਰੈਂਗੇ।।
ਕੋਟਿ ਸਨਾਨ ਗਜਾਦਿਕ ਦਾਨ ਅਨੇਕ ਸੁਅੰਬਰ ਸਾਜ ਬਰੈਂਗੇ।।
ਬ੍ਰਹਮ ਮਹੇਸਰ ਬਿਸਨ ਸਚੀਪਤਿ ਅੰਤ ਫਸੇ ਜਮ ਫਾਸ ਪਰੈਂਗੇ।।
ਜੋ ਨਰ ਸ੍ਰੀ ਪਤਿ ਕੇ ਪ੍ਰਸ ਹੈਂ ਪਗ ਤੇ ਨਰ ਫੇਰ ਨ ਦੇਹ ਧਰੈਂਗੇ।।੮।।੨੮।।

44. Tav Prasaad Savaiye

Maanav Indra Gajindra naraadhip jon trilok ko raaj karaingay.

Kot sanaan gajaadik daan anek savambar saaj baraingay.

Brahm mahesar bisan sachipat ant fasay jum faas paraingay.

Jay nar sripat kay pras hai pug tay nar fer na deh dharaingay. 8. 28 (14)

44. Tav Prasaad Savaiye

Men who possess mighty elephants become kings and rule over the whole world,

Men who take numerous ritual-baths and give in charity elephants and other animals and marry at special savambars,[1]

All these and even Brahma, Shiva, Vishnu and Indra shall at the end fall into the noose of Death.

But those who fall at the feet of God and seek His protection shall not go through the cycle of transmigration.[2] (14)

---

1. Special functions held in ancient times for the selection of marriage partners.
2. **Transmigration** is the cycle of birth, death and rebirth.

45. ਬਚਿਤ੍ਰ ਨਾਟਕ ਰਸਾਵਲ ਛੰਦ ॥

ਜਿਤੇ ਰਾਮ ਹੂਏ। ਸਭੈ ਅੰਤਿ ਮੂਏ। ਜਿਤੇ ਕਿਸਨ ਹ੍ਵੈ ਹੈ। ਸਭੈ ਅੰਤਿ ਜੈ ਹੈ ॥੭੦॥
ਜਿਤੇ ਦੇਵ ਹੋਸੀ। ਸਭੈ ਅੰਤ ਜਾਸੀ। ਜਿਤੇ ਬੋਧ ਹ੍ਵੈ ਹੈ। ਸਭੈ ਅੰਤਿ ਛੈ ਹੈ ॥੭੧॥
ਜਿਤੇ ਦੇਵਰਾਯੰ। ਸਭੈ ਅੰਤ ਜਾਯੰ। ਜਿਤੇ ਦਾਇਤ ਏਸੰ। ਤਿਤਯੋ ਕਾਲ ਲੇਸੰ ॥੭੨॥
ਨਰਸਿੰਘਾ ਵਤਾਰੰ। ਵਹੇ ਕਾਲ ਮਾਰੰ। ਬਡੋ ਡੰਡਧਾਰੀ। ਹਨਿਓ ਕਾਲ ਭਾਰੀ ॥੭੩॥
ਦਿਜੰ ਬਾਵਨੇਯੰ। ਹਨਿਯੋ ਕਾਲ ਤੇਯੰ। ਮਹਾਂ ਮੱਛ ਮੁੰਡੰ। ਫਧਿਓ ਕਾਲ ਝੁੰਡੰ ॥੭੪॥

45. Rasaval Chhand

Jitay Raam hooay, sabhai ant mooay;

Jitay Kisan huwai hai, sabhai ant jai hai. 71

Jitay dev hosee, sabhai ant jaasee

Jitay bodh huwai hai, sabhai ant chhai hai. 72

Jitay devaraayang, sabhai ant jaayang,

Jitay daeet esang, titio kaal lessang. 72

Nar singha vataarang vahay kaal marang,

Bado dand-dhari, hanio kaal bhaaree. 73

Dijang Bawaneyang, haniyo kaal teyang,

Maha machh mundang, fadio kaal jhundang. 74

45. BACHITRA NATAK

Rasaval Chhand

The Ramas, as many there were,
All came to an end.
And the Krishnas too
Couldn't last for ever. 70

Neither the angels stay, nor the Buddhas.
Neither the god of gods[1], nor the demons survive. 71-72

The incarnation, called Narsingha[2], Man-lion was also
    subject to Death.
So were the most powerful conquerors
    Destroyed by the All-powerful Time. 73

Bawan[3], The diminutive incarnation (of Vishnu),
    Was also smothered by Death. 74

---

1. God of gods, refers to Indra.
2. He killed king Harnaksh to save Bhagat Prahlad.
3. Incarnation of Vishnu.

46. ਸਵੱਯੇ ॥

ਤੋ ਤਨ ਤਿਆਗਤਹੀ, ਸੁਨਰੇ ਜੜ੍ਹ! 'ਪ੍ਰੇਤ' ਬਖਾਨ ਤ੍ਰਿਆ ਭਜਿ ਜੈ ਹੈ।
ਪੁਤ੍ਰ, ਕਲਤ੍ਰ ਸੁਮਿਤ੍ਰਸਖਾ, 'ਇਹ ਬੇਗ ਨਿਕਾਰਹੁ' ਆਇਸ ਦੈ ਹੈ।
ਭਉਨ, ਭੰਡਾਰ, ਧਰਾ ਗੜ੍ਹ, ਜੇਤਕ, ਛਾਡਤ ਪ੍ਰਾਨ ਬਿਗਾਨ ਕਹੈ ਹੈ।
ਚੇਤ ਰੇ ਚੇਤ! ਅਚੇਤ ਮਹਾ ਪਸੂ! ਅੰਤ ਕੀ ਬਾਰ ਅਕੇਲੋ ਈ ਜੈ ਹੈ।।੩੩।।

46. Savaiye

To tan tiyagat hi sunray jarh ! 'Pret' bakhaan triya bhaj jai hai.
Putr, kalitr, sumitr sakha,'Ih baig nikaarah' aais dai hai.
Bhaun bhandaar dharaa garh jetak chhadat praan bigaan kahai hai.
Chet ray chet ! Achet maha pas ! ant kee baar akelo ee jai hai. 33 (716)

46. Savaiye (Tatees Savaiye)

Listen, you ignorant one : As soon as you leave your body, your wife shall run away from you, calling you a 'ghost'.

Your sons, your wife, companions and fast friends shall all shout 'Make haste to take out the dead body'.[1]

As soon as you breathe your last, all your houses, treasures, land and forts will pass on to others.

Reflect and ponder, you great brute; you shall have to go alone in the end. (716)

---
1. In hot countries like India, dead bodies are generally disposed of within twenty four hours to avoid risk of putrefaction of decomposition.

47. ਅਕਾਲ ਉਸਤਤਿ ॥

ਕੋਊ ਭਇਓ ਮੁੰਡੀਆ ਸੰਨਿਆਸੀ, ਕੋਊ ਜੋਗੀ ਭਇਓ,
ਕੋਊ ਬ੍ਰਹਮਚਾਰੀ, ਕੋਊ ਜਤੀ ਅਨਮਾਨਬੋ ॥
ਹਿੰਦੂ ਤੁਰਕ ਕੋਊ ਰਾਫਜੀ ਇਮਾਮ ਸਾਫੀ, ਮਾਨਸ ਕੀ ਜਾਤ ਸਬੈ ਏਕੈ ਪਹਿਚਾਨਬੋ ।
ਕਰਤਾ ਕਰੀਮ ਸੋਈ ਰਾਜ਼ਕ ਰਹੀਮ ਓਈ, ਦੂਸਰੇ ਨ ਭੇਦ ਕੋਈ ਭੂਲ ਭ੍ਰਮ ਮਾਨਬੋ ॥
ਏਕ ਹੀ ਕੀ ਸੇਵ, ਸਭਹੀ ਕੋ ਗੁਰਦੇਵ ਏਕ, ਏਕ ਹੀ ਸਰੂਪ,
ਸਬੈ ਏਕੈ ਜੋਤ ਜਾਨਬੋ ॥੧੫॥੮੫॥

47. Akaal Ustat

Kou bhaiyo mundeeaa sanyasi kou jogi bhaio kou brahmchari kou jati unmaanbo.

Hindoo Turk kou Rafji Imaam safi maanas ki jaat sabhai ekai pahchaanbo.

Karta kareem soi Raazak Raheem oee, doosro na bhed koi bhool bharm maanbo.

Ek hi ki sev sabh hi ko Gurdev ek, ek hi saroop, sabhai ekai jot jaanbo.

15.85 (19)

SECTION V
UNIVERSAL BROTHERHOOD

47. (Akaal Ustat 15. 85)

Some one shaves his head and becomes a Sanyasi, another becomes a Yogi, another Brahmchari and yet another an ascetic.

Some are Hindus, others are Muslims, some are Rafjis, Imams and Safis, but all belong to the one race of humanity.

Karta[1] and Karim[2] are one and the same (God).

He is called a Razak,[3] and Rahim[3]; there is no difference; to think otherwise would be a mistake.

Worship only one God, who is the Supreme Guru of all, and regard His Form as one and His Light as pervading in all. (19)

---

1. The Hindus call God **Karta** which means the Creator.
2. The Muslims call God, **Karim** which means the Good.
3. The other names used by Muslims for God are **Razak**–the Sustainer and **Rahim**–the Compassionate.

48. ਅਕਾਲ ਉਸਤਤਿ ॥

ਦੇਹੁਰਾ ਮਸੀਤ ਸੋਈ ਪੂਜਾ ਔ ਨਿਵਾਜ ਓਈ,
ਮਾਨਸ ਸਬੈ ਏਕ ਪੈ ਅਨੇਕ ਕੋ ਭ੍ਰਮਾਉ ਹੈ ॥
ਦੇਵਤਾ ਅਦੇਵ ਜੱਛ ਗੰਧ੍ਰਬ ਤੁਰਕ ਹਿੰਦੂ,
ਨਿਆਰੇ ਨਿਆਰੇ ਦੇਸਨ ਕੇ ਭੇਸ ਕੋ ਪ੍ਰਭਾਉ ਹੈ ॥
ਏਕੈ ਨੈਨ ਏਕੈ ਕਾਨ ਏਕੈ ਦੇਹ ਏਕੈ ਬਾਨ,
ਖਾਕ ਬਾਦ ਆਤਸ ਔ ਆਬ ਕੋ ਰਲਾਉ ਹੈ ॥
ਅਲਹ ਅਭੇਖ ਸੋਈ ਪੁਰਾਨ ਔ ਕੁਰਾਨ ਓਈ,
ਏਕ ਹੀ ਸਰੂਪ ਸਬੈ ਏਕ ਹੀ ਬਨਾਉ ਹੈ ॥੧੬॥੮੬॥

48. Akaal Ustat

Dehuraa masit soee pooja oh nivaj oee,

maanas sabhai ek pai anek ko bhramaau hai.

Devta adev jachh gandharab Turk Hindoo,

niaray niaray desan kay bhes ko prabhaau hai.

Ekai nain ekai kaan ekai deh ekai baan,

khaak baad, aatas au aab ko ralaau hai.

Alah Abhekh soi, Puraan au Quran oee,

ek hi saroop sabhai ek hi banaau hai.

16.86 (19)

48. Akaal Ustat 16. 86

God is in the temple as well as in the mosque.

He is in the Hindu worship as well as in the Muslim prayer. All men are basically the same, though they appear different through our mistake.[1]

Deities, demons, heavenly musicians, Hindus and Muslims are all one, though they use different dresses according to the influence of regional customs.

All men have the same eyes, ears body and figure made out of the mixture of earth, air, fire and water.

The Abhekh (of the Hindus) and the Allah (of the Muslims) are one and the same, the Quran and the Puranas are His (praise). They are all of the same pattern; the one Lord had made them. (19)

---

[1] Religions should emphasise the Fatherhood of God and Brotherhood of man instead of differences in matters of worship, doctrine, ritual and dress.

49. ਅਕਾਲ ਉਸਤਤਿ ॥

ਜੈਸੇ ਏਕ ਆਗ ਤੇ ਕਨੂਕਾ ਕੋਟ ਆਗ ਉਠੇ,

ਨਿਆਰੇ ਨਿਆਰੇ ਹੁਇ ਕੈ ਫੇਰਿ ਆਗ ਮੋ ਮਿਲਾਹਿੰਗੇ ॥

ਜੈਸੇ ਏਕ ਧੂਰ ਤੇ ਅਨੇਕ ਧੂਰ ਪੂਰਤ ਹੈ,

ਧੂਰ ਕੇ ਕਨੂਕਾ ਫੇਰ ਧੂਰ ਹੀ ਸਮਾਹਿੰਗੇ ॥

ਜੈਸੇ ਏਕ ਨਦ ਤੇ ਤਰੰਗ ਕੋਟ ਉਪਜਤ ਹੈ,

ਪਾਨ ਕੇ ਤਰੰਗ ਸਬੈ ਪਾਨ ਹੀ ਕਹਾਹਿੰਗੇ ॥

ਤੈਸੇ ਬਿਸੁ ਰੂਪ ਤੇ ਅਭੂਤ ਭੂਤ ਪ੍ਰਗਟ ਹੋਇ,

ਤਾਹੀ ਤੇ ਉਪਜ ਸਬੈ ਤਾਹੀ ਮੈ ਸਮਾਹਿੰਗੇ ॥੧੯॥੮੨॥

49. Akaal Ustat

Jaisay ek aag tay kanooka kot aag uthhay,

niyaray niyaray hui kay fer aag mai milaahingay.

Jaisay ek dhoor tay anek dhoor poorat hai,

dhoor kay kanooka fer dhoor hi samaahingay.

Jaisay ek nad tay tarang kot upjat hai,

paan kay tarang sabhai paan hi kahaahingay.

Taisay bisu roop tay abhoot bhoot pragat hoi,

taahee tay upaj sabhai taahee mai samaahingay.

(19)

49. Akaal Ustat 17. 87

As out of a single fire, millions of sparks emerge and though separate, they come back again as they fall in the fire,

As out of a heap of dust, particles fly up filling the air, but soon they come down and fall in the same heap.

As out of a single river, numerous ripples rise up, but soon, being water, fall into the river again.

So from God spring non-living things and living beings, and as they come from Him shall all merge in Him again. (19)

50. ਸਵੱਯੇ ॥

ਜਾਗਤਿ ਜੋਤਿ ਜਪੈ ਨਿਸ ਬਾਸੁਰ, ਏਕ ਬਿਨਾ ਮਨ ਨੈਕ ਨ ਆਨੈ ।

ਪੂਰਨ ਪ੍ਰੇਮ ਪ੍ਰਤੀਤ ਸਜੈ, ਬ੍ਰਤ ਗੋਰ ਮੜੀ ਮਟ ਭੁਲ ਨ ਮਾਨੈ ॥

ਤੀਰਥ ਦਾਨ ਦਯਾ ਤਪ ਸੰਜਮ, ਏਕ ਬਿਨਾ ਨਹਿ ਏਕ ਪਛਾਨੈ ॥

ਪੂਰਨ ਜੋਤ ਜਗੈ ਘਟ ਮੈ, ਤਬ ਖਾਲਸ ਤਾਹਿ ਨਖਾਲਸ ਜਾਨੈ ॥੧॥

50. Savaiye

Jaagat Jot japai nis bassar, ek binaa mun naik na aanai.

Pooran prem pratit sajai, brat gor marhi mat bhool na maanai.

Teerath daan dayaa tup sanjam, ek binaa nah ek pachhaanai.

Pooran jot jagai ghat mai, tab Khaalis tah nakhaalis jaanai. 1. (712)

SECTION VI
THE KHALSA

50. Savaiye (Tatees Savaiye 1)

He (the Khalsa)[1] meditates on the Ever-radiant Light, day and night, and rejects all else but the One Lord from his mind.

He decorates himself with perfect love and faith and believes not in fasts, tombs, crematoriums and hermit-cells even by mistake.

He knows none except the One Lord in the performance of acts of pilgrimage, charities, compassion, austerity and self-control.

Such a man in whose heart shines the full Divinely radiant Light is a true and pure Khalsa. (712)

---

1. This hymn which defines the **Khalsa** was obviously composed by Guru Gobind Singh after the creation of the **Khalsa Brotherhood** in 1699. A.D.

51. ਸਵੱਯਾ (ਕ੍ਰਿਸ਼ਨਾਵਤਾਰ)

ਧੰਨ ਜੀਓ ਤਿਹ ਕੋ ਜਗ ਮੈ, ਮੁਖ ਤੇ ਹਰਿ, ਚਿਤ ਮੈ ਜੁਧੁ ਬਿਚਾਰੈ ॥
ਦੇਹ ਅਨਿੱਤ ਨ ਨਿੱਤ ਰਹੈ, ਜਸ ਨਾਵ ਚੜੈ ਭਵ ਸਾਗਰ ਤਾਰੈ ॥
ਧੀਰਜ ਧਾਮ ਬਨਾਇ ਇਹੈ ਤਨ, ਬੁਧਿ ਸੁ ਦੀਪਕ ਜਿਓ ਉਜਿਆਰੈ ॥
ਗਿਆਨਹਿ ਕੀ ਬਢਨੀ ਮਨਹੁ ਹਾਥ ਲੈ ਕਾਤਰਤਾ ਕੁਤਵਾਰ ਬੁਹਾਰੈ ॥੨੪੯੨॥੫੧੪॥

51. Savaiya (Krishanavtar)

Dhan jio tih ko jag mai, mukh tay Har, chit mai judh beechaarai.
Deh anit na nit rahay, jus naav charay bhav saagar taarai.
Dheeraj dhaam banai ihai tan, budh su deepak jiu ujiaarai.
Gian kee badhni manah haath lai, kaatartaa kutwaar buhaarai. (570)

51. Savaiya (Krishanavtar)

Blessed is the life of that person in the world[1] who recites the Holy Name with his mouth and contemplates war against evil in his mind.

He regards the body as a temporary vesture and uses the boat of the Lord's Name to cross the rough world-ocean.

He makes a closet of patience in the body and illumines the mind with the lamp of divine knowledge,

He takes up the broom of (spiritual) wisdom in his hands and sweeps away all cowardice and falsehood. (570)

---

1. Here is the concept of the **Ideal Man** of Guru Gobind Singh which was concretised by the creation of the **Khalsa**.

52. ਸਵੱਯਾ ॥

ਜੁਧ ਜਿਤੇ ਇਨਹੀ ਕੇ ਪ੍ਰਸਾਦਿ ਇਨਹੀ ਕੇ ਪ੍ਰਸਾਦਿ ਸੁ ਦਾਨ ਕਰੇ ॥
ਅਘ ਓਘ ਟਰੇ ਇਨਹੀ ਕੇ ਪ੍ਰਸਾਦਿ ਇਨਹੀ ਕੀ ਕ੍ਰਿਪਾ ਫੁਨਿ ਧਾਮ ਭਰੇ ॥
ਇਨਹੀ ਕੇ ਪ੍ਰਸਾਦਿ ਸੁ ਬਿਦਜਾ ਲਈ ਇਨਹੀ ਕੀ ਕ੍ਰਿਪਾ ਸਭ ਸੱਤ੍ਰੁ ਮਰੇ ॥
ਇਨਹੀ ਕੀ ਕ੍ਰਿਪਾ ਕੇ ਸਜੇ ਹਮ ਹੈ ਨਹੀਂ ਮੋ ਸੋ ਗਰੀਬ ਕਰੋਰ ਪਰੇ ॥੨॥

52. Savaiya

Judh jitay inahi kay prasaad, inahi kay prasaad su daan karay.
Agh ogh taray inahi kay prasaad, inahi ki kirpaa fun dhaam bharay.
Inahi kay prasaad su bidyaa laee, inahi ki kirpaa sabh satra maray.
Inahi ki kirpa kay sajay hum hain, nahi mo so gareeb kror paray. 2. (716)

52. Savaiya

It is through the actions of the Khalsa[1] that I have won all my victories and have been able to give charities to others.

It is through their help that I have overcome all sorrows and ailments and have been able to fill my house with treasures.

It is through their grace that I have got education, and through their assistance I have conquered all my enemies.

It is through their aid that I have attained this position, otherwise there are millions of unknown mortals like me. (716)

---

1. Guru Gobind Singh pays his tribute to the contribution and the achievement of the **Khalsa**.

53. ਸਵੱਯਾ ॥

ਸੇਵ ਕਰੀ ਇਨਹੀ ਕੀ ਭਾਵਤ ਔਰ ਕੀ ਸੇਵ ਸੁਹਾਤ ਨ ਜੀ ਕੋ ॥
ਦਾਨ ਦੀਯੋ ਇਨ ਹੀ ਕੋ ਭਲੋ ਅਰ ਆਨ ਕੋ ਦਾਨ ਨ ਲਾਗਤ ਨੀਕੋ ॥
ਆਗੈ ਫਲੈ ਇਨਹੀ ਕੋ ਦਯੋ ਜਗ ਮੈ ਜਸ ਔਰ ਦਯੋ ਸਭ ਫੀਕੋ ॥
ਮੋ ਗ੍ਰਿਹ ਮੈ ਮਨ ਤੇ ਤਨ ਤੇ ਸਿਰ ਲੌ ਧਨ ਹੈ ਸਭ ਹੀ ਇਨਹੀ ਕੋ ॥੩॥

53. Savaiya

Sev karee inahi ki bhaavat, aur ki sev suhaat na jee ko.
Daan deeyo inahi ko bhalo, ar aan ko daan na laagat neeko.
Aagay falay inahi ko dayo, jag mai jas aur dayo sabh feeko.
Mo grah mai man tay tan tay, sirr lo dhan hai sabh hi inahi ko. (717)

53. Savaiva

It is a great pleasure to serve them (the Khalsa)[1] for I do not regard the service of others as delightful to me.

It is beneficial to give them gifts, for granting favours to others, does not appear good to me.

Whatever is bestowed on them will bear fruit in the future and bring honour in this world; to give anything to others seems to be of litttle avail.

I dedicate (and bequeath) whatever is in my home, my body, my mind, my head, my wealth and all my belongings to them. (717)

---

1. Guru Gobind Singh's great love and respect for the Khalsa is expressed in this composition.

54. ਰਾਮਕਲੀ ਪਾਤਿਸ਼ਾਹੀ ੧੦ ॥

ਰੇ ਮਨ ਐਸੋ ਕਰਿ ਸੰਨਿਆਸਾ ॥

ਬਨ ਸੇ ਸਦਨ ਸਬੈ ਕਰਿ ਸਮਝਹੁ ਮਨ ਹੀ ਮਾਹਿ ਉਦਾਸਾ ॥੧॥ ਰਹਾਉ ॥

ਜਤ ਕੀ ਜਟਾ ਜੋਗ ਕੋ ਮੱਜਨੁ ਨੇਮ ਕੇ ਨਖਨ ਬਢਾਓ ॥

ਗਿਆਨ ਗੁਰੂ ਆਤਮ ਉਪਦੇਸਹੁ ਨਾਮ ਬਿਭੂਤ ਲਗਾਓ ॥੧॥

ਅਲਪ ਅਹਾਰ ਸੁਲਪ ਸੀ ਨਿੰਦ੍ਰਾ ਦਯਾ ਛਿਮਾ ਤਨ ਪ੍ਰੀਤਿ ।

ਸੀਲ ਸੰਤੋਖ ਸਦਾ ਨਿਰਬਾਹਿਬੋ ਹ੍ਵੈਬੋ ਤ੍ਰਿਗੁਣ ਅਤੀਤਿ ॥੨॥

ਕਾਮ ਕ੍ਰੋਧ ਹੰਕਾਰ ਲੋਭ ਹਠ ਮੋਹ ਨ ਮਨ ਸੋਂ ਲਜਾਵੈ ।

ਤਬ ਹੀ ਆਤਮ ਤਤ ਕੋ ਦਰਸੇ ਪਰਮ ਪੁਰਖ ਕਹ ਪਾਵੈ ॥੩॥੧॥

54. Ramkali Patshahi Dasvee

Ray man aiso kar sanyaasaa.

Bun say sadan sabhai kar samjhah man hi maah udaasa.

Jat ki jattaa jog ko majjan nem kay nakhan badhaao.

Gian guru aatam upadesah naam bibhoot lagaao.1.

Alap ahaar sulap si nindraa dayaa chhimaa tan preet.

Seel santokh sadaa nirbaahbo huwaibo trigun ateet. 2.

Kaam krodh hankaar lobh hathh moh na man sou lyavay.

Tab hi aatam tat ko darsay param purakh kah pavai. 3.1 (709)

SECTION VII
YOGA

54. Shabad Hazare Ramkali 3.1

O man! Practise renunciation in this manner,

Regard your house as a forest (retreat) and live as a hermit in your heart. Pause.

Make countenance your matted hair, communion with God your bath, and performance or religious duties the growing of long nails.

Make divine knowledge your religious preceptor, enlighten your own soul and smear your body with the ashes of God's Name.

Eat little and sleep little; love the practice of compassion and forbearance.

Be calm and contented and thus you will gain freedom from the Three States.[1]

Keep your mind away from lust, anger, pride, greed, obstinacy and worldly love.

Thus you will see the essence of your own soul and also realise the Supreme Lord. (709)

---

1. The Three States are Rajas, Tamas, Satva. Rajas implies energy, desire and attachment and causes people to do work. Tamas implies ignorance and sloth and makes people lazy. Satva implies goodness and purity and promotes the pursuit of knowledge, creative arts and healthy living.

55. ਰਾਮਕਲੀ ਪਾਤਿਸ਼ਾਹੀ ੧੦ ॥

ਰੇ ਮਨ ਇਹ ਬਿਧਿ ਜੋਗੁ ਕਮਾਓ ॥
ਸਿੰਙੀ ਸਾਚ ਅਕਪਟ ਕੰਠਲਾ ਧਿਆਨ ਬਿਭੂਤ ਚੜ੍ਹਾਓ ॥੧॥ ਰਹਾਉ ॥
ਤਾਤੀ ਗਹੁ ਆਤਮ ਬਸਿ ਕਰ ਕੀ ਭਿੱਛਾ ਨਾਮ ਅਧਾਰੰ ॥
ਬਾਜੇ ਪਰਮ ਤਾਰ ਤਤੁ ਹਰਿ ਕੋ ਉਪਜੈ ਰਾਗ ਰਸਾਰੰ ॥੧॥
ਉਘਟੈ ਤਾਨ ਤਰੰਗ ਰੰਗਿ ਅਤਿ ਗਿਆਨ ਗੀਤ ਬੰਧਾਨੰ ॥
ਚਕਿ ਚਕਿ ਰਹੇ ਦੇਵ ਦਾਨਵ ਮੁਨਿ ਛਕਿ ਛਕਿ ਬਯੋਮ ਬਿਵਾਨੰ ॥੨॥
ਆਤਮ ਉਪਦੇਸ ਭੇਸੁ ਸੰਜਮ ਕੋ ਜਾਪੁ ਸੁ ਅਜਪਾ ਜਾਪੈ ॥
ਸਦਾ ਰਹੈ ਕੰਚਨ ਸੀ ਕਾਯਾ ਕਾਲ ਨ ਕਬਹੂੰ ਬਯਾਪੈ ॥੩॥੨॥

55. Ramkali Patshahi Dasvee

Ray man ih bidh jog kamaao.
Singee saach akapt kanthlaa dhian bibhoot charhaao. 1.Rahau.
Taatee gah aatam bas kar kee, bhichhaa naam adharang.
Baajay param taar tat Har ko upajai raag rasaarang. 1.
Ughtay taan tarang rung at gian geet bandhaanang.
Chak chak rahay dev danav mun chhak chhak biyom bivanang. 2.
Aatam updes bhes sanjam ko jaap su ajapaa jaapay.
Sadaa rahay kanchan si kaaya kaal na kabahoo biyapay. 3. 2   (710)

55. Shabad Hazare, Ramkali 3.2

O man ! Practise yoga in this way.

Make truth your horn[1], integrity your necklace and apply the ashes of meditation to your body. Pause.

Make the control of the mind your harp and the support of the Holy Name your alms.

Play the charming strings of God's Name so as to produce the delightful divine melody.

Vibrations of sweet tunes will create the waves of blissful music of divine knowledge.

Thus the gods, demons and ascetics will be wonder-struck and the riders of celestial chariots will become divinely intoxicated.

O Yogi, instruct your soul, wear the uniform of self-disciplne and remember God's Name silently and continuously in your own heart.

Thus your body will always shine like gold and the demons of death will not frighten you. (710)

---

1. These are references to the Yogi's paraphernalia like horn, necklace, ashes, harp, etc.

56. ਸਵੱਯੇ ॥

ਧਿਆਨ ਲਗਾਇ ਠਗਿਓ ਸਬ ਲੋਗਨ ਸੀਸ ਜਟਾ ਨਖ ਹਾਥ ਬਢਾਏ।
ਲਾਇ ਬਿਭੂਤ ਫਿਰਿਓ ਮੁਖ ਉਪਰ, ਦੇਵ ਅਦੇਵ ਸਬੈ ਡਹਿਕਾਏ।
ਲੋਭ ਕੇ ਲਾਗੇ ਫਿਰਿਓ ਘਰ ਹੀ ਘਰ, ਜੋਗ ਕੇ ਨਿਆਸ ਸਬੈ ਬਿਸਰਾਏ।
ਲਾਜ ਗਈ ਕਛੁ ਕਾਜ ਸਰਿਓ ਨਹਿ, ਪ੍ਰੇਮ ਬਿਨਾ ਪ੍ਰਭ ਪਾਨ ਨ ਆਏ ॥੧੮॥

56. Savaiye

Dhian lagaaai thagio sabh logan, sees jataa nakh haath badaae.
Lai bibhoot firio mukh oopar, dev adev sabai dhahikaae.
Lobh kay laagay firio ghar hi ghar, jog kay niyaas sabai bisraae.
Laaj gaee kichh kaaj sariyo nah, prem binaa Prabh paan na aaye. 18.
(715)

56. Savaiye (Tatees Saviye)

The Yogi, by show of meditation, the growth of matted locks[1] on the head, long nails on the fingers has deceived all people.

He, by applying ashes on his face and roaming hither and thither, has duped the gods (good people) and demons (bad people).

He, overwhelmed by greed has gone from house to house (to collect alms) and forgotten the code of discipline (contentment) of true Yoga.

He has lost all his self-respect and missed the goal; without real devotion God can never be realised.

(715)

---

1. These are references to the Yogi's paraphernalia, like matted locks, long nails, ashes etc.

57. ਬਚਿਤ੍ਰ ਨਾਟਕ ॥ ਦੋਹਰਾ

ਤਿਨ ਬੇਦੀਅਨ ਕੇ ਕੁਲ ਬਿਖੇ ਪ੍ਰਗਟੇ ਨਾਨਕ ਰਾਇ।
ਸਭ ਸਿਖਨ ਕੋ ਸੁਖ ਦਏ ਜਤ ਤਤ ਭਏ ਸਹਾਇ ॥੪॥

ਚੌਪਈ।

ਤਿਨ ਇਹ ਕਲ ਮੇ ਧਰਮੁ ਚਲਾਯੋ। ਸਭ ਸਾਧਨ ਕੋ ਰਾਹੁ ਬਤਾਯੋ।
ਜੋ ਤਾਕੇ ਮਾਰਗ ਮਹਿ ਆਏ। ਤੇ ਕਬਹੂੰ ਨਹਿ ਪਾਪ ਸੰਤਾਏ ॥੫॥
ਜੋ ਜੋ ਪੰਥ ਤਵਨ ਕੇ ਪਰੇ। ਪਾਪ ਤਾਪ ਤਿਨਕੇ ਪ੍ਰਭ ਹਰੇ।
ਦੂਖ ਭੂਖ ਕਬਹੂੰ ਨ ਸੰਤਾਏ। ਜਾਲ-ਕਾਲ ਕੇ ਬੀਚ ਨ ਆਏ ॥੬॥
ਨਾਨਕ ਅੰਗਦ ਕੋ ਬਪੁ ਧਰਾ। ਧਰਮ ਪ੍ਰਚੁਰਿ ਇਹ ਜਗ ਮੇ ਕਰਾ।
ਅਮਰ ਦਾਸ ਪੁਨਿ ਨਾਮੁ ਕਹਾਯੋ। ਜਿਨੁ ਦੀਪਕ ਤੇ ਦੀਪ ਜਗਾਯੋ ॥੭॥
ਜਬ ਬਰ ਦਾਨਿ ਸਮੈ ਵਹੁ ਆਵਾ। ਰਾਮਦਾਸ ਤਬ ਗੁਰੂ ਕਹਾਵਾ।
ਤਿਹ ਬਰ ਦਾਨਿ ਪੁਰਾਤਨਿ ਦੀਆ। ਅਮਰਦਾਸਿ ਸੁਰਪੁਰਿ ਮਗੁ ਲੀਆ ॥੮॥

57. Bachitar Naatak
Doharaa

Tinn Bediyan kay kul bikhai pragatay Nanak Rai
Sabh Sikhan so sukh dayay jut tut bhaey sahaai.

Chaupai

Tin ih kal me dharam chalaayo, sabh saadhan ku raah bataaiyo.
Jo taakay maarag mah aae, te kabahoo nah paah santaae. 5
Jo jo panth tavan kay paray, paap taap tinkay prabh haray.
Dookh bhookh kabhoo na santaae. Jaal- kaal kay beech na aae.
Nanak Angad ko bap dharaa, dharam prachur ih jug main karaa.
Amardaas pun naam kahayo, jin deepak te deep jagaaio. 7
Jab bar daan samai vah aavaa, Raamdaas tah Guru kahaavaa.
Tah bar daan puraatan deeaa, Amardaas surpur mug leeaa. 8

57. BACHITAR NATAK
Doharaa

In the house of the Bedis was born Nanak, the king of kings, who brought joy to his followers and became their refuge. Both here and in the hereafter.4

Chaupai

He established Religion in this dark age,
And showed the Path to all men of faith.
He who accepted his Way,
Was afflicted not by sin.5

He who followed in his footsteps,
Him affected neither sin nor sorrow.
He was delivered of pain and hunger,
And was trapped not thereafter by death 6.

Then, Nanak adopted Angad's form,
And spread this Religion far and wide.
Then, he was known as Amar Das,
As one light kindles another. 7

And when came time for the fulfilment of his blessing,
He was called Ram Das, the Guru.
It was in fulfilment of an old command (of God).
And, then, Amar Das returned to the heavenly abode. 8.

ਸ੍ਰੀ ਨਾਨਕ ਅੰਗਦਿ ਕਰਿ ਮਾਨਾ। ਅਮਰ ਦਾਸ ਅੰਗਦ ਪਹਿਚਾਨਾ।
ਅਮਰ ਦਾਸ ਰਾਮਦਾਸ ਕਹਾਯੋ। ਸਾਧਨ ਲਖਾ ਮੂੜ੍ਹ ਨਹਿ ਪਾਯੋ।।੯।।
ਭਿੰਨ ਭਿੰਨ ਸਭ ਹੂੰ ਕਰਿ ਜਾਨਾ। ਏਕ ਰੂਪ ਕਿਨਹੂੰ ਪਹਿਚਾਨਾ।
ਜਿਨ ਜਾਨਾ ਤਿਨ ਹੀ ਸਿਧਿ ਪਾਈ। ਬਿਨ ਸਮਝੇ ਸਿਧਿ ਹਾਥਿ ਨ ਆਈ।।੧੦।।
ਰਾਮਦਾਸ ਹਰਿ ਸੋ ਮਿਲਿ ਗਏ। ਗੁਰਤਾ ਦੇਤ ਅਰਜਨਹਿ ਭਏ।
ਜਬ ਅਰਜਨ ਪ੍ਰਭ ਲੋਕਿ ਸਿਧਾਏ। ਹਰਿ ਗੋਬਿੰਦ ਤਿਹਠੀ ਠਹਰਾਏ।।੧੧।।
ਹਰਿਗੋਬਿੰਦ ਪ੍ਰਭ ਲੋਕਿ ਸਿਧਾਰੇ। ਹਰੀ ਰਾਇ ਤਿਹਠਾਂ ਬੈਠਾਰੇ।
ਹਰੀ ਕ੍ਰਿਸਨਿ ਤਿਨ ਕੇ ਸੁਤ ਵਏ। ਤਿਨ ਤੇ ਤੇਗ ਬਹਾਦੁਰ ਭਏ।।੧੨।।

Sri Nanak Angad kar maanaa, Amardaas Angad pahchaanaa
Amardaas Ramdaas kahaiyo, sadhan lakha moor nahee paayo. 9
Bhin bhin sabh hoo kar jaanaa, ek roop kinahoo pahchaanaa.
Jin jaanaa tinahee sidh paaee, bin samjhay sidh haath na aaee. 10
Ramdaas Har so mil gaey, gurtaa det Arjunah bhaey.
Jab Arjun Prabh lok sidhaaey, Har Gobind tinhi thhahiraaey.11
Hargobind Prrabh lokh sidhaarey, Hari rai tihathhaa baithharay.
Hari Krishan tin kay sut vaey, Tin te Teg Bahaadur bha-ay. 12

It was Nanak, the venerable, who was known as Angad.
Thereafter, it was Amar Das who assumed the form of Ram Das.
All this is known to men of faith; but the fools know not the mystery. 9

They distinguish and separate one from the other.
And rare is the one who knows that they, indeed, were one.
They who realised this in their hearts, attained Realisation (of God).
But they who understood it not, were at fault. 10

Ram Das, then, merged in God,
Appointing Arjun as the Guru.
And when Arjun returned to the heavens,
He established Har Gobind in his place. 11

When Har Gobind proceeded to the Abode of God,
It was Har Rai who took his place.
After him came Hari Krishan, his son,
And then it was Teg Bahadur who succeeded him. 12.

58. ਬਚਿਤ੍ਰ ਨਾਟਕ

ਤਿਲਕ ਜੰਞੂ ਰਾਖਾ ਪ੍ਰਭ ਤਾ ਕਾ॥
ਕੀਨੋ ਬਡੋ ਕਲੂ ਮਹਿ ਸਾਕਾ॥
ਸਾਧਨਿ ਹੇਤ ਇਤੀ ਜਿਨਿ ਕਰੀ॥
ਸੀਸੁ ਦੀਆ ਪਰ ਸੀ ਨ ਉਚਰੀ॥੧੩॥
ਧਰਮ ਹੇਤ ਸਾਕਾ ਜਿਨਿ ਕੀਆ।
ਸੀਸ ਦੀਆ ਪਰ ਸਿਰਰ ਨ ਦੀਆ॥
ਨਾਟਕ ਚੇਟਕ ਕੀਏ ਕੁਕਾਜਾ॥
ਪ੍ਰਭ ਲੋਗਨ ਕਹ ਆਵਤ ਲਾਜਾ॥੧੪॥

ਦੋਹਰਾ

ਠੀਕਰਿ ਫੋਰਿ ਦਿਲੀਸਿ ਸਿਰਿ, ਪ੍ਰਭ ਪੁਰ ਕੀਆ ਪਯਾਨ॥
ਤੇਗ ਬਹਾਦਰ ਸੀ ਕ੍ਰਿਆ, ਕਰੀ ਨ ਕਿਨਹੂੰ ਆਨ॥੧੫॥
ਤੇਗ ਬਹਾਦਰ ਕੇ ਚਲਤ, ਭਯੋ ਜਗਤ ਕੋ ਸੋਕ।
ਹੈ ਹੈ ਹੈ ਸਭ ਜਗ ਭਯੋ, ਜੈ ਜੈ ਜੈ ਸੁਰ ਲੋਕ॥੧੬॥

58. BACHITAR NATAK

Tilak janjhoo rakhaa prabh taa kaa,
keeno bado kaloo mai saakaa.
Saadhan het itee jin karee,
Sees deeaa pur see na ucharee. 13
Dharam het saakaa jin keeaa.
Sees deeaa pur sirar na deeaa
Naatak chetak keeay kukaajaa,
Prabh logan kah aavat laajaa. 14.

Doharaa

Thheekar forh dilees sir, Prabh pur keeaa payaan,
Teg Bahadur see kirya, karee na kinahoo aan. 15.
Teg Bahaadur ke chalat, bhayo jagat ko sok,
Hai hai hai sabh jag bhayo, jai jai jai sur lok. 16.

58. BACHITAR NATAK

Guru Teg Bahadur was the protector of the tilak (forehead mark) and Janeu (the sacred thread) of the Hindus.
He performed a unique act in the age of Kali; He made the supreme sacrifice for the sake of the men of other faith.
He gave his head without a groan ; 13
He did this deed to defend Dharma.
He gave up his head but not his resolve.
Making antics and performing tricks (miraclas),
Is considered disgraceful by holy men. 14

Doharaa

Casting off his bodily vesture on the head of Suzerain of Delhi;
He departed to the Realm of God.
None who came into the world performed such glorious deeds as he. 15
Teg Bahadur produccd dismay in the world
This world cried, "Alas, Alas !
The Heaven rings with greetings of victory. 16

59. ਬਚਿਤ੍ਰ ਨਾਟਕ ॥ ਚੌਪਈ ॥

ਅਬ ਮੈ ਅਪਨੀ ਕਥਾ ਬਖਾਨੋ ॥ ਤਪ ਸਾਧਤ ਜਿਹ ਬਿਧਿ ਮੁਹਿ ਆਨੋ ॥
ਹੇਮ ਕੁੰਟ ਪਰਬਤ ਹੈ ਜਹਾਂ ॥ ਸਪਤ ਸਿੰਗ ਸੋਭਿਤ ਹੈ ਤਹਾਂ ॥੧॥
ਸਪਤ ਸਿੰਗ ਤਿਹ ਨਾਮੁ ਕਹਾਵਾ ॥ ਪੰਡ ਰਾਜ ਜਹ ਜੋਗ ਕਮਾਵਾ ॥
ਤਹ ਹਮ ਅਧਿਕ ਤਪੱਸਿਆ ਸਾਧੀ ॥ ਮਹਾ ਕਾਲ ਕਾਲਕਾ ਅਰਾਧੀ ॥੨॥
ਇਹ ਬਿਧਿ ਕਰਤ ਤਪਸਿਆ ਭਯੋ ॥ ਦ੍ਵੈ ਤੇ ਏਕ ਰੂਪ ਹ੍ਵੈ ਗਯੋ ॥
ਤਾਤ ਮਾਤ ਮੁਰ ਅਲਖ ਅਰਾਧਾ ॥ ਬਹੁ ਬਿਧਿ ਜੋਗ ਸਾਧਨਾ ਸਾਧਾ ॥੩॥
ਤਿਨ ਜੋ ਕਰੀ ਅਲਖ ਕੀ ਸੇਵਾ ॥ ਤਾ ਤੇ ਭਏ ਪ੍ਰਸੰਨਿ ਗੁਰਦੇਵਾ ॥
ਤਿਨ ਪ੍ਰਭ ਜਬ ਆਇਸ ਮੁਹਿ ਦੀਆ ॥ ਤਬ ਹਮ ਜਨਮ ਕਲੂ ਮਹਿ ਲੀਆ ॥੪॥
ਚਿਤ ਨ ਭਯੋ ਹਮਰੋ ਆਵਨ ਕਹ ॥ ਚੁਭੀ ਰਹੀ ਸ੍ਰੁਤਿ ਪ੍ਰਭ ਚਰਨਨ ਮਹਿ ॥
ਜਿਉ ਤਿਉ ਪ੍ਰਭ ਹਮ ਕੋ ਸਮਝਾਯੋ ॥ ਇਮ ਕਹਿਕੈ ਇਹ ਲੋਕ ਪਠਾਯੋ ॥੫॥

59. BACHITAR NATAK

Chaupai

Ab mai apni kathaa bakhaano Tap saadhat jih bidh muh aano.
Hemkunt parbat hai jahaa Sapat sring sobhat hai tahaa. 1.
Sapat sring tih naam kahaavaa, Pand raaj jah jog kamaavaa.
Tab hum adhik tapasiyaa sadhi, Mahaa kaal kaalkaa araadhi. 2.
Ih bidh karat tapaisyaa bhayo, Duvai tay ek roop huvai gayo.
Taat maat mur Alakh araadhaa, Bah bidh jog saadhanaa sadhaa. 3
Tin jo kari Alakh ki sewaa, Ta tay bhae prasan Gurdevaa.
Tin Prabh jab aais muh Deeyaa, Tab hum janam, kaloo mai leeyaa. 4
Chit na bhayo hamro aavan kah, Chubhi rahee surt Prabh charnan mah.
Jiu tiu Prabh ham ko samjhaaio, Im kahkay ih lok pathhaaio. 5.

SECTION VIII
AUTOBIOGRAPHICAL

59. BACHITAR NATAK

Chaupai

Now I relate my own story,
How God sent me into the world, while I was absorbed in meditation,
On the site of Hemkunt mountain,
Where the seven peaks shine in glory. 1
That spot is known as Sapt Sring.
Where Pandav kings practised yoga,
There I put in much spiritual effort.
I prayed to God–the Lord of Death. 2.
Thus I continued my meditations,
And became merged in the Divine Being.
My father and mother also worshipped the Indescribable One,
And carried out in various ways several spiritual practices. 3.
Because they served God with great devotion
He–the Supreme Guru–was much pleased.
When God gave me His Command,
I was born in this age of Kalyuga.[1] 4.
My mind was not happy in coming to the world,
Because it was attached to the feet of the Lord.
Somehow, God explained to me His purpose,
And sent me to this world, with His directive. 5.   (54)

---

1. It means the dark age–the period of sin and corruption.

60. ਬਚਿਤ੍ਰ ਨਾਟਕ ।। ਚੌਪਈ ।।

ਇਹ ਕਾਰਨਿ ਪ੍ਰਭ ਮੋਹਿ ਪਠਾਯੋ ।। ਤਬ ਮੈ ਜਗਤ ਜਨਮੁ ਧਰਿ ਆਯੋ ।।
ਜਿਮ ਤਿਨ ਕਹੀ ਇਨੈ ਤਿਮ ਕਹਿ ਹੌਂ ।। ਔਰ ਕਿਸੂ ਤੇ ਬੈਰ ਨ ਗਹਿ ਹੌਂ ।।੩੧।।
ਜੋ ਹਮ ਕੋ ਪਰਮੇਸਰ ਉਚਰਿ ਹੈ । ਤੇ ਸਭ ਨਰਕ ਕੁੰਡ ਮਹਿ ਪਰਿ ਹੈ ।।
ਮੋ ਕੌ ਦਾਸੁ ਤਵਨ ਕਾ ਜਾਨੋ ।। ਯਾ ਮੈ ਭੇਦ ਨ ਰੰਚ ਪਛਾਨੋ ।।੩੨।।
ਮੈ ਹੌ ਪਰਮ ਪੁਰਖ ਕੋ ਦਾਸਾ ।। ਦੇਖਨ ਆਯੋ ਜਗਤ ਤਮਾਸਾ ।।
ਜੋ ਪ੍ਰਭ ਜਗਤਿ ਕਹਾ ਸੋ ਕਹਿਹੌਂ ।। ਮ੍ਰਿਤ ਲੋਕ ਤੇ ਮੋਨਿ ਨ ਰਹਿਹੌਂ ।।੩੩।।

60. BACHITAR NATAK
Chaupai

Ih kaaran Prabh moh pathhaayo . Tab mai jagat janam dhar aayo.

Jim tin kahi inai tim kah ho. Aur kisoo tay bair na gah ho. 31

Jay hum ko Parmesar uchar hai, Tay sabh narak kund mah par hai.

Mo ko daas tavan kaa jaano, Yaa mai bhed no runch pachhaano. 32

Mai ho Param Purakh ko daasaa. Dekhan aayo jagat tamaasaa.

Jo Prabh jagat kahaa so kahiho. Mirta lok tay mon na rahiho. 33

60. BACHITAR NATAK

Chaupai

For this purpose God sent me.

Then I was born and came into this world.

I tell you what God told me;

I have no enmity with any one. 31

Those who call me God

Will fall into the pit of Hell.

Regard me as a servant of the Lord.

Do not have any doubt about it. 32.

I am the slave of the Supreme Being;

I have come to witness the world-drama[1] ;

I tell the people what God told me then;

I shall not keep silent on account of the fear of mortals. 33.   (57)

---

1. Guru Gobind Singh is the only prophet who has written his own autobiography in poetic form, entitled 'Bachitar Natak' (the Wonderful Drama).

61. ਬਚਿਤ੍ਰ ਨਾਟਕ ॥ ਚੌਪਈ ॥

ਹਮ ਇਹ ਕਾਜ ਜਗਤ ਮੋ ਆਏ ॥
ਧਰਮ ਹੇਤ ਗੁਰਦੇਵ ਪਠਾਏ ॥
ਜਹਾਂ ਤਹਾਂ ਤੁਮ ਧਰਮ ਬਿਥਾਰੋ ॥
ਦੁਸਟ ਦੋਖੀਯਨਿ ਪਕਰਿ ਪਛਾਰੋ ॥੪੨॥
ਯਾਹੀ ਕਾਜ ਧਰਾ ਹਮ ਜਨਮੰ ॥
ਸਮਝਿ ਲੇਹੁ ਸਾਧੂ ਸਬ ਮਨਮੰ ॥
ਧਰਮ ਚਲਾਵਨ ਸੰਤ ਉਬਾਰਨ ॥
ਦੁਸਟ ਸਭਨ ਕੋ ਮੂਲ ਉਖਾਰਨ ॥੪੩॥

61. BACHITAR NATAK

Chaupai

Hum eh kaaj jagat mo aay.

Dharam het Gurdev pathhaay.

Jaha taha tum Dharam bithaaro.

Dust dokhian pakar pachhaaro. 42.

Yahi kaaj dharaa hum janmang.

Samajh leh sadhu sabh manmang.

Dharam chalaavan sant ubaaran

Dust sabhan ko mool ukhaaran. 43

(57)

61. BACHITAR NATAK

Chaupai

I have come into this world for this purpose,

The Supreme Guru has sent me for the protection of Righteousness :

'You should propagate righteousness everywhere; Seize and destroy the sinful and the wicked.'¹ 42.

I have taken birth for this purpose,

Let the holy men understand this in their minds.

I have come for spreading Divine religion and for protection of saints,

And for annihilating (uprooting) all the tyrants. 43. (57)

---

1. This was the two fold mission of the Tenth Guru—to uphold righteounsess and to punish the unrighteous.

62. ਬਿਚਿਤ੍ਰ ਨਾਟਕ–ਅਪਨੀ ਕਥਾ
ਚੌਪਈ

ਮੁਰਪਿਤ ਪੂਰਬਿ ਕਿਯਸਿ ਪਯਾਨਾ। ਭਾਂਤਿ ਭਾਂਤਿ ਕੇ ਤੀਰਥਿ ਨ੍ਹਾਨਾ।
ਜਬ ਹੀ ਜਾਤਿ ਤ੍ਰਿਬੇਣੀ ਭਏ। ਪੁੰਨ ਦਾਨ ਦਿਨ ਕਰਤ ਬਿਤਏ॥੧॥
ਤਹੀ ਪ੍ਰਕਾਸ਼ ਹਮਾਰਾ ਭਯੋ। ਪਟਨਾ ਸ਼ਹਰ ਬਿਖੈ ਭਵ ਲਯੋ।
ਮਦ੍ਰ ਦੇਸ ਹਮ ਕੋ ਲੇ ਆਏ। ਭਾਂਤਿ ਭਾਂਤਿ ਦਾਈਅਨ ਦੁਲਰਾਏ॥੨॥
ਕੀਨੀ ਅਨਿਕ ਭਾਂਤਿ ਤਨ-ਰੱਛਾ। ਦੀਨੀ ਭਾਂਤਿ ਭਾਂਤਿ ਕੀ ਸਿੱਛਾ।
ਜਬ ਹਮ ਧਰਮ ਕਰਮ ਮੋ ਆਏ। ਦੇਵਲੋਕਿ ਤਬ ਪਿਤਾ ਸਿਧਾਏ॥੩॥

62. BACHITAR NATAK
Chaupai

Murpat poorab kiyus piaanaa, bhant bhant kay teerath naanaa.
Jab hee jaat trabenee bha-ay, punn daan din karat bita-ay.1
Tahee prakaash hamaaraa bhayo, Patnaa shahar bikhai bhav layo.
Madra des hum ko lai aa-ay, bhant bhant daaeeun durlaa-ay.2
Keenee anak bhant tun rachhaa, deenee bhant bhant kee sichhaa,
Jab hum dharam karam mo aai, devlok tab pitaa sidhaa-ay.3

62. BACHITAR NATAK

Chaupai (13)

When my father departed for the East, he went to all places of pilgrimage. When he reached Triveni,[1] for many days he distributed charities and did other meritorious acts. There was I conceived and, later, took birth in the city of Patna. Afterwards, I was taken to the Panjab, where I was fondled and nursed with great affection and care. My body was tended in every way, and I got instruction in every branch of knowledge. And when I was of an age fit to perform my religious functions, my father left for the Heavenly Abode.[2]

---

1. The place where the three rivers—Ganga, Jamuna and Saraswati meet near Allahabad.
2. Guru Gobind Singh was nine years old when his father was martyred in 1675.

63. ਬਚਿਤੁ ਨਾਟਕ*
ਰਸਾਵਲ ਛੰਦ

ਜਬੈ ਬਾਣ ਲਾਗਿਓ। ਤਬੈ ਰੋਸ ਜਾਗਿਓ।
ਕਰ ਲੈ ਕਮਾਣੰ। ਹਨੰ ਬਾਣ ਤਾਣੰ।।੩੧।।
ਸਬੈ ਬੀਰ ਧਾਏ। ਸਰੋਘੰ ਚਲਾਏ।
ਤਬੈ ਤਾਕਿ ਬਾਣੰ। ਹਨਿਓ ਏਕ ਜੁਆਣੰ।।੩੨।।
ਹਰੀ ਚੰਦ ਮਾਰੇ। ਸੁ ਜੋਧਾ ਲਤਾਰੇ।
ਸੁ ਕਾਰੋੜ ਰਾਜੰ। ਵਹੈ ਕਾਲ ਘਾਜੰ।।੩੩।।
ਰਣੰ ਤਿਆਗਿ ਭਾਗੇ। ਸਬੈ ਤ੍ਰਾਸ ਪਾਗੇ।
ਭਈ ਜੀਤ ਮੇਰੀ। ਕ੍ਰਿਪਾ ਕਾਲ ਤੇਰੀ।।੩੪।।
ਰਣੰ ਜੀਤਿ ਆਏ ਜਯੰ ਗੀਤ ਗਾਏ।
ਧਨੰਧਾਰ ਬਰਖੇ। ਸਬੈ ਸੂਰ ਹਰਖੇ।।੩੫।।

63. BACHITAR NATAK

Rasaaval Chhand

Jabai baan lagio, tabai ros jaagio;
Kar lai kamaanang, hanang baan taanang. 31
Sabhai beer dhaaye, saroghang chalaaye,
Tabai taak bannang, hanio ek juanang. 32
Hari chand maaray, su jodhaa lataaray,
Su karor raayang, vahay kaal ghaaiyang. 33
Ranang tiyaag bhaagay, sabhai traas paagay,
Bhaee jeet meree, kirpa kaal teree. 34
Ranang jeet aaiye, jayang geet gaaye,
Dhandhaar barkhay, sabai soor harkhay. 35.

* ਭੰਗਾਣੀ ਜੁਧ

63. BACHITAR NATAK

Rasaaval Chhand (31-35)

When I felt the touch of the arrow, my wrath was kindled.
I took up the bow in my hand and showered my arrows upon the enemy. The enemy advanced towards me, with a shower of arrows. Then I aimed an arrow and struck one of them dead. Hari Chand too fell at my hands and another prince called Karor and many chiefs fell dead, and others fled the field in panic,
I won a decisive battle. O God, it was through your favour that I won. We sang the songs of victory. All my heroes were pleased and I rewarded them with much wealth.

64. ਬਚਿਤ੍ਰ ਨਾਟਕ (ਸਰਬ ਕਾਲ ਕੀ ਬੇਨਤੀ) ਅਪੁਨੀ ਕਥਾ ਚੌਪਈ ॥

ਸਰਬਕਾਲ ਸਭ ਸਾਧ ਉਬਾਰੇ ।
ਦੁਖੁ ਦੈ ਕੈ ਦੋਖੀ ਸਭ ਮਾਰੇ ॥
ਅਦਭੁਤਿ ਗਤਿ ਭਗਤਨ ਦਿਖਰਾਈ ।
ਸਭ ਸੰਕਟ ਤੇ ਲਏ ਬਚਾਈ ॥੧॥
ਸਭ ਸੰਕਟ ਤੇ ਸੰਤ ਬਚਾਏ ।
ਸਭ ਕੰਟਕ ਕੰਟਕ ਜਿਮ ਘਾਏ ।
ਦਾਸ ਜਾਨ ਮੁਰਿ ਕਰੀ ਸਹਾਇ ।
ਆਪ ਹਾਥ ਦੈ ਲਯੋ ਬਚਾਇ ॥੨॥
ਅਬ ਜੋ ਜੋ ਮੈ ਲਖੇ ਤਮਾਸਾ ।
ਸੋ ਸੋ ਕਰੋ ਤੁਮੈ ਅਰਦਾਸਾ ॥
ਜੋ ਪ੍ਰਭ ਕ੍ਰਿਪਾ ਕਟਾਕ੍ਸ਼ਿ ਦਿਖੈ ਹੈ ।
ਸੋ ਤਵ ਦਾਸ ਉਚਾਰਤ ਜੈ ਹੈ ॥੩॥

64. BACHITAR NATAK APNI KATHAA
Chaupai

Sarab-kaal sabh saadh ubaray,

Dukh dai kai dokhee sabh maaray,

Adbhut gut bhagtan dikhraaee,

Sabh sankat te laye bachaaee. 1.

Sabh sankat te sant bachaae,

Sabh kantak kantak jim ghaaye,

Daas jaan mur karee sahaai.

Aap hathh dai layo bachaai. 2

Ab jo jo mai lakhay tamaasaa,

So so karo tumai Ardaasaa.

Jo prabh kirpaa kataachh dikhai hai,

So tav daas uchaarat jai hai. 3.

64. BACHITAR NATAK

Chaupai. (1-3)

God saves all His Saints in all ages. And; He gives pain to and destroys all their detractors. The devotees are a witness to His miracles who keeps them safe from all harm.

The Saints are ever protected from all harm : they who stand in their way are swept off like thorns. God protected me, too, taking me to be His Slave and gave me His Hand and became my refuge. O God, all the play that I have witnessed so far I have rendered upto you. All your Mercies and Miracles your servant has uttered before you. 3.

65. ਖ਼ਿਆਲ ਪਾਤਿਸ਼ਾਹੀ ੧੦ ॥

ਮਿਤ੍ਰ ਪਿਆਰੇ ਨੂੰ ਹਾਲ ਮੁਰੀਦਾਂ ਦਾ ਕਹਿਣਾ ॥
ਤੁਧੁ ਬਿਨੁ ਰੋਗੁ ਰਜਾਈਆਂ ਦਾ ਓਢਣ ਨਾਗ ਨਿਵਾਸਾ ਦੇ ਰਹਿਣਾ ॥
ਸੂਲ ਸੁਰਾਹੀ ਖੰਜਰੁ ਪਿਆਲਾ ਬਿੰਗ ਕਸਾਈਆਂ ਦਾ ਸਹਿਣਾ ।
ਯਾਰੜੇ ਦਾ ਸਾਨੂੰ ਸੱਥਰੁ ਚੰਗਾ ਭਠ ਖੇੜਿਆ ਦਾ ਰਹਿਣਾ ॥੧॥੧॥

65. Khayal Patshahi Dasvee

Mitr piyaray noo haal mureedaa daa kahinaa.

Tudh bin rog rajaaia daa odhan naag nivaasaa day rahinaa.

Sool suraahi khanjar piyalaa bing kasaaiyaa daa sahinaa.

Yararay daa saanoo sathar changaa bhathh kheriaa daa rahinaa 1.6.

(711)

65. Khayal (Shabad Hazare)

Please tell the dear friend–the Lord–the plight of his disciples.[1]

Without you, the use of rich blankets is like a disease for us and the comfort of the house is like living with snakes.

Our water–pitchers are like stakes of torture and our cups have edges like daggers. Your neglect is like what animals suffer when they face butchers.

Our Beloved Lord's straw-bed is more pleasing to us than living in costly furnace-like urban houses. 1.6. (711)

---

1. This hymn is said to be composed by Guru Gobind Singh in the Machhiwara jungle in 1704.

66. ਜ਼ਫ਼ਰ ਨਾਮਹ

ਬਿਬਾਯਦ ਤੁ ਦਾਨਸ਼ ਪਰਸਤੀ ਕੁਨੀ॥
ਬ ਕਾਰੇ ਸ਼ੁਮਾ ਚੇਰਹ ਦਸਤੀ ਕੁਨੀ॥੭੭॥
ਚਿਹਾਂ ਸ਼ੁਦ ਕਿ ਚੁੰ ਬੱਚਗਾਂ ਕੁਸ਼ਤਹ ਚਾਰ॥
ਕਿ ਬਾਕੀ ਬਿਮਾਂਦਸਤੁ ਪੇਚੀਦਹ ਮਾਰ॥੭੮॥
ਚਿ ਮਰਦੀ ਕਿ ਅਖ਼ਗਰ ਖ਼ਮੋਸ਼ਾਂ ਕੁਨੀ॥
ਕਿ ਆਤਸ਼ ਦਮਾਰਾ ਬਦਉਰਾ ਕੁਨੀ॥੭੯॥
ਚਿ ਖ਼ੁਸ਼ ਗੁਫ਼ਤ ਫ਼ਿਰਦੌਸੀਏ ਖ਼ੁਸ਼ ਜ਼ੁਬਾਂ॥
ਸ਼ਿਤਾਬੀ ਬਵਦ ਕਾਰ ਆਹਰ ਮਨਾ॥੮੦॥

66. Zafar Namah

Bibaayad tu daanash parasti kuni,
Ba kaaray shumaa cherah dasti kuni. 77.
Chihaa shud ki choon bachgaa kushtah chaar.
Ki bakee bimadast pechidah maar. 78
Chi mardee ki akhgar khamoshaa kuni,
Ki aatash damaaraa badauraa kuni. 79
Chi khush guft Firdosiay khush zuba,
Shitabee bavad kaar aahar mannaa. 80.   (1392)

66. Zafar Namah*, 77-80

You (Emperor Aurangzeb) use your wisdom and act quickly;

Do reply to this letter as early as possible. 77.

What did it matter if you killed my four sons?[1]

After all the hooded Cobra (like me)[2] is still living to punish you. 78.

What manliness is it to extinguish some burning coal,

When the raging fire is spreading in all directons ? 79.

How beautifully the Persian poet (Firdausi) has summed it up :

'The evil-minded act quickly, thus hastening their doom.' 80.   (1392)

---

* This means " Letter of Victory", written by Guru Gobind Singh and addressed to Aurangzeb.

1. Guru Gobind Singh's reference is to his four sons who died at the hands of Aurangzeb's army and agents, Ajit Singh and Jujhar Singh died fighting against the Mughal army in the battle of Chamkaur, while Zorawar Singh and Fateh Singh were bricked alive by Wazir Khan, Governor of Sirhind in 1704.
2. This is a reference of the remarks of one of the courtiers of Wazir Khan who advised the killing of the two infant-children of Guru Gobind Singh, comparing them to the off-spring of a cobra.

67. ਚੰਡੀ ਚਰਿਤ੍ਰ।। ਸਵੱਯਾ।।

ਦੇਹ ਸਿਵਾ ਬਰ ਮੋਹਿ ਇਹੈ ਸੁਭ ਕਰਮਨ ਤੇ ਕਬਹੂ ਨ ਟਰੋਂ।।
ਨ ਡਰੋਂ ਅਰਿ ਸੋਂ ਜਬ ਜਾਇ ਲਰੋਂ ਨਿਸਚੈ ਕਰ ਆਪਨੀ ਜੀਤ ਕਰੋਂ।।
ਅਰੁ ਸਿਖ ਹੋਂ ਆਪਨੇ ਹੀ ਮਨ ਕੋ ਇਹ ਲਾਲਚ ਹਉ ਗੁਨ ਤਉ ਉਚਰੋਂ।।
ਜਬ ਆਵ ਕੀ ਅਉਧ ਨਿਦਾਨ ਬਨੈ ਅਤ ਹੀ ਰਨ ਮੈ ਤਬ ਜੂਝ ਮਰੋਂ।।੨੩੧।।

67. Chandi Charitra Savaiya

Deh Siva bar moh ihai, subh karman tay kabahoo na taroo.

Na daroo ur soo jab jaah laroo, nischay kar apnee jeet karoo.

Ar Sikh hoo apnay hı mun ko, ih laalach hau guna tau uchroo.

Jab aav kee audh nidhaan banay, ut hi run mai tab joojh maroo, 231 (99)

SECTION IX

SUPPLICATION

67. Chandi Charitra Savaiya, 231

Grant me this boon[1], O Lord[2]. that I may never be deterred from doing good deeds.

I should have no fear of the enemy,

When I go to battle and turn victory to my side. Let one directive guide my mind exclusively,

That I may ever be zealously singing Thy praises ;

And when the time comes, I should die, fighting heroically on the field of battle[3]. (99)

---

1. This hymn was the favourite prayer of Guru Gobind Singh.
2. The Guru uses the word **Shiva** for God. The Guru prays to the Almighty and not the Hindu deity bearing this name.
3. Heroic death on the field of battle is the goal of Guru Gobind Singh and the Khalsa.

68. ਸਵੈਯਾ ਪਾਤਸ਼ਾਹੀ ੧੦ (ਚੰਡੀ ਚਰਿਤੁ)

ਹੇ ਰਵਿ, ਹੇ ਸਸਿ, ਹੇ ਕਰੁਣਾਨਿਧ,
ਮੇਰੀ ਅਬੈ ਬਿਨਤੀ ਸੁਨ ਲੀਜੈ ॥
ਔਰ ਨ ਮਾਂਗਤ ਹਉ ਤੁਮ ਤੇ ਕਛੁ,
ਚਾਹਤ ਹੋ ਚਿਤ ਮੈ ਸੋਈ ਕੀਜੈ ॥
ਸ਼ਸਤ੍ਰਨ ਸੋਂ ਅਤਿ ਹੀ ਰਣ ਭੀਤਰ,
ਜੂਝ ਮਰੋ ਤਉ ਸਾਚ ਪਤੀਜੈ ॥
ਸੰਤ ਸਹਾਇ ਸਦਾ ਜਗ ਮਾਹਿ,
ਕ੍ਰਿਪਾ ਕਰ ਸਯਾਮ ਇਹੈ ਬਰ ਦੀਜੈ ॥੧੯੦੦॥੪੪੬॥

68. Savaiyaa Patshahi Dasvee

Hay rav, hay sas, hay karnaa nidh,
Meri abai binti sun leejai
Aur na maangat hau tum te kachh,
Chahat ho chit mai soee keejai.
Shastran so at hee runn bheetar,
Jhoojh maro tau saach pateejai,
Sant sahaai sadaa jag maah,
Kirpaa kar syam ihai bar deejai. 1900/446

68. Savaiye Patshahi Dasvee Chandi Charitra

Hear, O Merciful Lord ! the Light of all Lights.

This be my only supplication :

Let my mission be fulfilled ;

Let my life be a sacrifice unto

Righteousness is an action-packed battle-field of life culminating into a complete merger with Truth.

O the Helper of the Saints and All Pervading, grace me with your Blessing.

69. ਕਬਿਯੋਬਾਚ ਬੇਨਤੀ ॥ ਚੌਪਈ ॥

ਹਮਰੀ ਕਰੋ ਹਾਥ ਦੈ ਰੱਛਾ ॥
ਪੂਰਨ ਹੋਇ ਚਿਤ ਕੀ ਇੱਛਾ ॥
ਤਵ ਚਰਨਨ ਮਨ ਰਹੈ ਹਮਾਰਾ ॥
ਅਪਨਾ ਜਾਨ ਕਰੋ ਪ੍ਰਿਤਪਾਰਾ ॥
ਹਮਰੇ ਦੁਸਟ ਸਭੈ ਤੁਮ ਘਾਵਹੁ ॥
ਆਪ ਹਾਥ ਦੈ ਮੋਹਿ ਬਚਾਵਹੁ ॥
ਸੁਖੀ ਬਸੈ ਮੋਰੋ ਪਰਿਵਾਰਾ ॥
ਸੇਵਕ ਸਿੱਖ ਸਭੈ ਕਰਤਾਰਾ ॥੨॥

69. Kabio Baach Benti Chaupai

Hamaree karo haath dai rachhaa,
Pooran hoi chitt ki ichhaa.
Tav charnan mun rahai hamaaraa,
Apnaa jaan karo pritpaaraa. 1.
Humray dusht sabhai tum ghaavah,
Aap hathh dai moh bachaavah,
Sukhee basai moro parvaaraa,
Sewak Sikh sabhai kartaaraa. 2.

69. Chaupai

O God ! Protect me with Your helping hand,
And fulfil all the desires of my mind.
May my mind ever seek the shelter of your feet;

O Lord ! cherish me as Your own. 1.
O God, knock off all my enemies,
And preserve me with Your own hand.
May all my family feel happy (with your blessing),
Along with all my devotee-Sikhs and my followers. 2.

70. ਵਾਰ ਭਗਉਤੀ ਕੀ ਪਾਤਿਸ਼ਾਹੀ ੧੦ ॥
ਪਉੜੀ ॥

ਪ੍ਰਿਥਮ ਭਗਉਤੀ ਸਿਮਰਕੈ ਗੁਰੁ ਨਾਨਕ ਲਈ ਧਿਆਇ ।
ਅੰਗਦ ਗੁਰੁ ਤੇ ਅਮਰਦਾਸ, ਰਾਮਦਾਸੈ ਹੋਈ ਸਹਾਇ ।
ਅਰਜਨ ਹਰਿਗੋਬਿੰਦ ਨੋ, ਸਿਮਰੋ ਸ੍ਰੀ ਹਰਿਰਾਇ ।
ਸ੍ਰੀ ਹਰਿ ਕ੍ਰਿਸ਼ਨਿ ਧਿਆਇਐ, ਜਿਸੁ ਡਿਠੇ ਸਭ ਦੁਖ ਜਾਇ ।
ਤੇਗ ਬਹਾਦਰ ਸਿਮਰੀਐ, ਘਰਿ ਨੌਨਿਧ ਆਵੈ ਧਾਇ ।
ਸਭ ਥਾਈਂ ਹੋਇ ਸਹਾਇ ॥੧॥

70. Vaar Bhagauti Ki. Patshahi Dasvee
Pauri

Pritham Bhagauti simarkay, Guru Nanak laee dhiaai.
Angad Guru te Amardaas, Ramdaasay hoee sahaai.
Arjan Hargobind no, simaro Sri Har Rai,
Sri Har Krishan dhiaaeai, jis dithhai sabh dukh jaai
Teg Bahaadur simareeai ghar nau-nidh aavai dhaai.
Sabh thhaaee hoi sahaai. 1. (154)

70. Var Bhagauti Chandi-Di-Var

First call on God, the All-powerful,[1]
and then call on Nanak, the Guru.
And then on Angad, and Amardas, and Ramdas -
May they ever protect us and be our refuge !
And, then, call on Guru Arjan, and on Har Gobind, and Sri Hari Rai,
And, then, on Sri Har Krishan.
seeing whom all our woes come to an end.
And, then, call on Tegh Bahadur, the Guru,
Who brings the nine treasures[1] hastening to our home.
O God, be you ever with us wherever we be !

---

1. Nine Treasures refers to the traditional nine kinds of precious stones. Another interpretation is that the first nine gurus are the nine treasures.